THE LIBRARY O
CONTEMPORARY TH(

*America's most original voices
tackle today's most provocative issues*

PETE HAMILL

NEWS IS A VERB
*Journalism at the End of the
Twentieth Century*

"With the usual honorable exceptions, newspapers are getting dumber. They are increasingly filled with sensation, rumor, press-agent flackery, and bloated trivialities at the expense of significant facts. The Lewinsky affair was just a magnified version of what has been going on for some time. Newspapers emphasize drama and conflict at the expense of analysis. They cover celebrities as if reporters were a bunch of waifs with their noses pressed enviously to the windows of the rich and famous. They are parochial, square, enslaved to the conventional pieties. The worst are becoming brainless printed junk food. All across the country, in large cities and small, even the better newspapers are predictable and boring. A movie director once said of a certain screenwriter: 'He aspired to mediocrity, and he succeeded.' Many newspapers are succeeding in the same way."

NEWS IS A VERB

Journalism at the End of the Twentieth Century

PETE HAMILL

THE LIBRARY OF CONTEMPORARY THOUGHT
THE BALLANTINE PUBLISHING GROUP • NEW YORK

The Library of Contemporary Thought
Published by The Ballantine Publishing Group

Copyright © 1998 by Deidre Enterprises, Inc.

http://www.randomhouse.com

Library of Congress Cataloging-in-Publication Data
Hamill, Pete, 1935–
News is a verb / Pete Hamill. —1st ed.
p.   cm.
ISBN 0-345-42528-6 (alk. paper)
1. Journalism—United States—History—20th century.   I. Title.
PN4867.H36   1998
071'.3'0904—dc21   98-5896
                                                           CIP

Text design by Holly Johnson
Cover design by Ruth Ross
Cover photo © Marco Monti/Photonica

Manufactured in the United States of America

First Edition: April 1998

10   9   8   7   6   5   4   3   2   1

*This book is in memory of the following men and women,
journalists all, who were killed doing their jobs in Vietnam,
Cambodia, and Laos*

Arpin, Claude	Kusaka, Akira
Bailly, Francis	Laramy, Ronald B.
Bellendorf, Dieter	Laurent, Michel
Birch, Michael	Leandri, Paul
Bun Ly, Thun	Lekhi, Ramnik
Burrows, Larry	Miller, Gerald
Cantwell, John	Mine, Hiromishi
Capa, Robert	Mongkol, Tou Chhom
Caron, Gilles	My, Huynh Thanh
Castan, Sam	Noonan Jr., Oliver E.
Chan, Nun	Pigott, Bruce S.
Chapelle, Dickey	Potter, Kent
Chellappah, Charles	Reese, Everette
Colne, Roger	Reynolds, Terry L.
Dara, Chan	Rose, Jerry
Eggleston, Charles R.	Sakai, Kojiro
Ellison, Robert J.	Sakai, Tatsuo
Ezcurra, Ignacio	Savanuck, Paul D.
Fall, Bernard	Sawada, Kyoichi
Faye, Sam Kai	Schuyler, Philippa Duke
Flynn, Sean	Shimamoto, Keisaburo
Frosch, J. Frank	Shimkin, Alexander
Gallagher, Ronald D.	Stone, Dana
Hangen, Welles	Sully, François
Herbert, Gerard	Syvertsen, George
Hirons, Alan	Takagi, Yujiro
Huet, Henri	Takano, Isao
Hung Cuong, Duong	Van Thiel, Pieter R.
Ichinose, Taizo	Vichith, Sou
Ishii, Tomoharu	Wakabayashi, Hiroo
Ishiyama, Koki	Waku, Yoshihiko
Khoo, Terry	Yanagisawa, Takeshi
Kolenberg, Bernard	

Source: The Freedom Forum Journalists Memorial, Washington D.C.

Introduction

THIS IS NOT an objective or neutral essay. The subject
is so deeply entwined with my life that I can't write
about it in a cold, detached manner. Quite simply, I love
newspapers and the men and women who make them.
Newspapers have given me a full, rich life. They have
provided me with a ringside seat at some of the most extraordinary events in my time on the planet. They have
been my university. They have helped feed, house, and
educate my children. I want to them to go on and on
and on.

The newspaper that gave me my life was the *New
York Post*, as published by a remarkable, idiosyncratic
woman named Dorothy Schiff and edited by a tough,
smart, old-style newspaperman named Paul Sann. I started
there on June 1, 1960, working the night side as a reporter. The *Post* was then, and is now, a tabloid. That
blunt little noun has a pejorative quality these days, but
"tabloid" really is a neutral word, describing the shape of

the page. "Tabloid" can't, with any accuracy, describe the style, content, or intentions of *Newsday*, the *National Enquirer*, the *Rocky Mountain News*, the *New York Daily News*, the *Boston Herald*, the *Star*, the *New York Post*, the *Philadelphia Daily News*, or the *Globe*. All are published in tabloid format. But the *Star*, the *National Enquirer*, and the *Globe* are supermarket weeklies, whose basic goal is to entertain their readers, usually with tales of celebs-in-trouble. The rest are dailies, engaged in the traditional effort to inform their readers about their city, their nation, and the world. All tabloids are different, shaped by separate traditions and geographies. The daily newspapers that have endured—tabloid or broadsheet—are those that best serve the communities in which they are published. But the supermarket weeklies don't serve communities; they are national publications driven by an almost primitive populism. Like the mass-circulation Fleet Street tabloids that are their models, they are really about class. Their unsubtle message is as primitive as an ax: Don't feel so bad about your life, lady, these rich and famous people are even more miserable than you are.

So there are tabloids, and there are tabloids. I'm proud to have spent most of my working life as a tabloid man at the *Post*, the *New York Daily News*, and *New York Newsday*. At the *Post*, I served my apprenticeship—covering fires and murders, prizefights and riots—and did so in the best of company. Reporters in those days were not as well educated as they are now. Some were degenerate gamblers. Some had left wives and children in distant towns, or told husbands they were going for a bottle of milk and ended up back on night rewrite on a different coast. Some of them were itinerant boomers who worked brilliantly for six months and then got drunk, threw a typewriter out a window, and moved on. Some were tough veterans of the depression and World War II and were sour on the whole damned human race. But all of them were serious about the craft. And oh, Lord—were they fun.

It was their pride that they could turn out a fine, tough, tight newspaper with a fifth of the staff of the *New York Times*, and do it with great style. Let the *Times* be the New York Philharmonic; they were happy to play in the Basie band. They understood, and accepted, the limitations placed upon them by the tabloid format. Because space was very tight, every word must count. The headlines must sparkle. The photographs must add to the story, not simply illustrate it. And every story must have a *dramatic* point. There was no room for detailed analysis of the collapse of manufacturing in New York; you had to find a factory that was closing and a proud man or woman who might never work again. You couldn't just report a fire; you had to tell us about the people whose baby pictures and wedding albums had gone up, literally, in smoke. You had to look for good guys and bad guys, whenever they existed, and then save them from being cartoons with skepticism and doubt. Sometimes they slopped over into sentimentality or its twin brother, sensationalism, by expressing emotions they didn't feel. Most of the time, they were content to adopt a hard-boiled cynical manner, accompanied by a wink.

All of them were conscious of their limitations; they knew that they never once had turned out an absolutely perfect newspaper, because the newspaper was put out by human beings. But in their separate ways, they tried very hard never to write anything that would bring the newspaper shame. They would be appalled at the slovenly way the word "tabloid" is now used. They didn't pay whores for stories. They didn't sniff around the private lives of politicians like agents from the vice squad. Even in large groups, on major stories, the photographers didn't behave like a writhing, snarling, mindless centipede, all legs and Leicas, falling upon some poor witness like an instrument of punishment. Somehow, they found ways to get the story without behaving like thugs or louts.

Perhaps because Murray Kempton seemed always to be among them, they had decent manners. Kempton was writing a column for the *Post* when I first came around, and it was like having Henry James in the city room. He was more than just a great reporter; he saw the world with his own private vision. At the newspaper, he talked to everybody, from editors to copyboys, trying out lines for the column, the talk always brilliant and ironical, the manner democratic. In person or in print, the Kempton style was as full of surprises as a solo by John Coltrane. He proved in his art and his life that a tabloid man could have the guts of a burglar and the grace of a saint. He died in 1997, still working for a tabloid, and at his funeral I heard more than one mourner say that he improved all of us just by showing up.

So did a man named Ted Poston. In the early 1950s, he became the first black reporter at a mainstream daily in New York. That paper was the *Post*. Over and over again, he went to the American South alone, in the years when it wasn't easy to be black and alone in that heartbreaking region with a notebook in your hand. He was chased down mean roads by Klansmen. He was physically threatened while covering the trial of some white morons who had murdered a black teenager named Emmet Till for the terrible crime of whistling at a white woman. He had endured the usual stupid slights, North and South, but he remained a man of grace and generosity, particularly to those of us who were young.

"This is the best gahdamned business in the world," he told me once. "We help more gahdamned people than any gahdamned government. So don't you ever disgrace it, you hear me?"

I hear him still. Ted Poston was a proud, funny *tabloid* newspaperman. And I can't imagine him pursuing a Princess Di or a Madonna along some midnight street to find out the names of their boyfriends. He wouldn't stay very long at a newspaper whose basic menu was a gluey mixture of celebrities-in-trouble and rewritten press releases. He'd be outraged if you lumped him with the *Star* and the *Enquirer*. He was a serious man. He wanted to help people. He felt he was doing more good than any gahdamned government.

Such men were my instructors. They taught me and hundreds of others about how to work at an honorable craft and perhaps even how to live. Many of us went on to the big broadsheets and had glittering careers. Some became historians, or screenwriters, or educators, or movie directors. We see each other from time to time, far from the grimy old city room of the *New York Post*, and we talk like people always do when they have shared some of the happiest times of their lives. We had all been baptized in the bracing waters of the tabloid world; we carried that experience with us like a badge of honor.

My own journey took me to other newspapers, to the writing of novels, to literally millions of words of journalism. In 1993, I worked for five wonderful weeks as editor in chief of the *New York Post* in the collective effort to save that newspaper from extinction. We succeeded. Rupert Murdoch bought the newspaper, and I was immediately replaced as editor. I didn't care; the paper lived. In 1997, I became editor in chief of the *New York Daily News*. I tried very hard to put everything I knew about New York and the craft of tabloid journalism into that newspaper. The broad goals were very simple. We would insist on quality reporting, writing, and photography; we would respect the intelligence of our readers; we would make a serious, sustained effort to attract more women and more immigrants to the newspaper. The publisher had other ideas. After eight months, I was gone. This time I did care. Not about myself; in some ways, getting fired was a liberation. But I cared about the people on the staff. Most were there when I arrived. I had hired others. Some were very young; some were middle-aged. I had tried to convince all of them, without issuing manifestos or making city-room speeches, that together we were going to put out the best goddamned tabloid in history. We were on our way. We didn't get to finish the job.

I mention all this because I hope that what follows is not glibly dismissed as the sour residue of a major disappointment. It isn't. I want all newspapers to thrive, including those that broke my heart.

But I'm deeply troubled by what is happening to so many American newspapers in the final years of the twentieth century. I'm saddened by the way "tabloid" has been transformed into an adjective, usually followed by the noun "trash." I'm appalled by the way so many newspapers have abandoned certain fundamental responsibilities, in the name of giving readers what publishers, in their omniscience, think those readers want.

For me, the health and vitality of newspapers are far more important than my own minuscule part in their history. To begin with, I am a citizen of this country. I believe that all those noble clichés about newspapers are even truer now than they were in the past. Without good newspapers, operating primarily as instruments of knowledge, we cannot truly function as a healthy, continuously evolving democracy. In the age of the ten-second spot, the superficialities of political coverage on television, the sometimes hysterical urgencies of the twenty-four-hour cable news cycle, the blather of talk radio, the unedited paranews of the Internet, newspapers are essential to our political discourse. And they are more than that.

On a local level, they can be an annealing agent in the contemporary American city, with its extraordinary racial, religious, and ethnic diversity. In their coverage of sports and entertainment, they are critical to the nation's wider culture, high and low. For immediacy, they can no longer compete with the technology of television, but they can be a solid corrective to the enormous flaws and dangers of that immediacy. At the same time, through their advertising, they are important to the economies of cities; they post the signs at the entrance to the capitalist bazaar.

But I am writing this during some of the most wretched weeks for newspapers in my memory. The Lewinsky affair was the first major news story to break in the era that combines the Internet, twenty-four-hour news cycles on cable television, and the relaxation—or cheapening—of standards in major newspapers. The allegations that President Clinton had had a sexual relationship with a twenty-one-year-old intern named Monica Lewinsky—and urged her to lie about it under oath—exploded like a mega-media bomb. The three network anchors flew home from Havana, where the Pope was visiting with Fidel Castro. CNN planted Wolf Blitzer in a permanent spot on the White House lawn. For the first time in months, MSNBC canceled all bulletins, panel discussions, and E-mail referenda on the JonBenet Ramsey murder case and went on a war footing in Washington, D.C. Countless messages flew around the Internet, where the story had broken on an amateur gossip 'zine called the Drudge Report. The right-wing regulars of talk radio burst into hosannas, almost tearful with gratitude. Hour after hour, the airwaves were slippery with rumor, innuendo, unattributed quotes from vague and shadowy sources. Lurid details were retailed as if they were confirmed fact: a semen-stained dress, lavish gifts, late-night appointments. Someone located an innocuous piece of footage showing a starry-eyed Ms. Lewinsky being hugged by President Clinton for a few seconds in the midst of a campaign crowd. It was played over and over and over; it was used as a logo; it was blown up in newspapers. In the days that followed, I saw it more than I ever saw the Zapruder film, the piece of amateur footage that showed President John F. Kennedy being shot in the Dallas motorcade on November 22, 1963.

This should have been a great moment for newspapers to assert their now most useful function on a breaking story: to take a long breath, start reporting, separate fact from rumor, and verify or debunk the details of stories. They failed miserably. Even the *Washington Post*, the *New York Times*, and the *Wall Street Journal* operated most of the time as if the basic story was true, and that William Jefferson Clinton was only days away from resigning in disgrace. Yes, the accounts were sprinkled with the good old reliable word "alleged." There were many sentences that started with the phrase "the allegations, if true . . ." But it seemed obvious that nobody in the media believed the president. There were comically Talmudic readings of Clinton's few statements. When he said that there *is* no sexual relationship was he admitting that there *was* a sexual relationship? There were pumped-up rehashes of the Paula Jones case, with replays of her accusations against Clinton. Poor Gennifer Flowers was hauled out of the lounge of American public life. And the great Matt Drudge of the Drudge Report—how Dickens would have cherished that name!—did a star turn on *Meet the Press*.

On one of these days in the fever zone, January 26, the *New York Post* and the *New York Daily News* had identical front-page headlines: "CAUGHT IN THE ACT." The giant letters stated baldly that a Secret Service agent had walked in on the president and Ms. Lewinsky while they were having sex. Sure, there were a few lines leading into the headlines, about Kenneth Starr probing a report that they were . . . "CAUGHT IN THE ACT." But there was no qualifying question mark attached to either headline. The provenance of the story was a blurred "sources said." The readers were not told whether these were White House sources, sources close to the special prosecutor, or sources friendly to Ms. Lewinsky. It was just "sources said." Those same "sources" claimed that a Secret Service man saw Clinton and Lewinsky engaging in an "intimate act." (This same fellow was referred to again, deep in the *Daily News* story, as a "tryst witness," apparently a new Washington job category.) In their account of the same tale, CNN added a factlet placing the president and the intern alone in the basement theater of the White House residence.

All of this salacious soap opera was built upon those vague "sources." That word could have covered the kid delivering Chinese food or someone from FedEx or a wandering campaign contributor who had slept late in the Lincoln bedroom. Unfortunately, there was one big problem. It wasn't true. Within a day, the story had been withdrawn by the *Dallas Morning News*, from which it had sprung, the withdrawal shrouded in ambiguous rhetorical fog. There were no headlines the next day that said: *"NOT* CAUGHT IN THE ACT."

Nothing much was learned by some editors. Nine days later, on February 4, the Internet edition of the *Wall Street Journal* moved a story about a fifty-year-old White House steward named Bayani Nelvis, who had worked at the White House for eighteen years under four presidents. The steward was said to have told the grand jury that he saw the president and Ms. Lewinsky together in the Oval Office, "according to one person familiar with the event." The *Journal* story went on to cite "two individuals familiar with Nelvis's testimony," who claimed that the steward "reported recovering tissues with lipstick and other stains on them after the alleged meeting between Clinton and Lewinsky and that he disposed of them in the kitchen-pantry." The same sources claimed that Nelvis reported this to the Secret Service because he "was personally offended" by it.

This report moved on the *Journal's* Web site at about 4 P.M. As the *New York Times* later reported: "Within minutes after the first story was posted on the Internet, the *Journal's* Washington bureau chief, Alan Murray, was on CNBC, a cable television news channel, talking about the *Journal's* scoop. His remarks were later picked up by MSNBC and posted on the MSNBC Web site."

As stained presidential tissues flew around in cyberspace, the original story was being revised. An attorney for Nelvis named Joseph Small attacked the *Journal's* report as "absolutely false and irresponsible." He declined to go into detail about what Nelvis did say but insisted that Nelvis didn't mention lipstick or other stains on tissues. His remarks were included in the print edition of the *Journal.* In the February 9 Internet edition, an article ran under the headline "Steward Denies Seeing Clinton and Monica Lewinsky Alone."

The story began: "White House steward Bayani Nelvis told a grand jury he didn't see President Clinton alone with Monica Lewinsky, contrary to a report in the *Wall Street Journal* last week."

In the fourth paragraph, *Journal* managing editor Paul Steiger said, "We deeply regret our erroneous report of Mr. Nelvis's testimony."

Meanwhile, of course, the story had flown around the country, been picked up by some wire services (but not, to its credit, the Associated Press), printed in many newspapers, used as jaw fodder on talk shows, and incorporated into the lurid mythology of the scandal. The *Journal's* final story, with its apology, ran on page A24.

The need for solid, even sober newspaper reporting was made even more urgent by the quality of the television coverage. It was appalling: breathless young reporters talking in italics; wild charges qualified only by the phrase "if true"; sneering don't-try-to-bullshit-us confrontations with the White House press secretary at his daily briefings. By the second day, there was incessant speculation about impeachment or resignation, a point that was reached in the Watergate affair only after many, many months of dogged reporting and public hearings. In almost all discussion of the Lewinsky affair, and underlying all the "reporting," there was an assumption of guilt. Dots were being connected that didn't connect. Gravity was almost totally missing. We had reached some turning point in American journalism: The president of the United States was being examined with the tools usually reserved for the likes of Joey Buttafuoco.

There was, of course, a huge audience for all of this—at least in the early days. Ratings went up. Newspapers sold more copies than usual. But then something odd began to happen. The president's approval ratings went higher than ever. When reporters used photo opportunities with Palestinian leader Yasir Arafat and British prime minister Tony Blair to harass the president with sex-scandal questions, they looked obsessed, petty, even vindictive, and certainly guilty of bad manners. Many citizens were saying that even "if true," they didn't care about the charges against the president. A majority expressed contempt for the special prosecutor. And a huge majority said they were furious with the media. Television and newspapers had gone over the top. They had blown the story way out of proportion. They had printed too many rumors as if they were facts.

A brief period of self-examination followed: panel discussions, tentative mea culpas. Many journalists seemed genuinely surprised. They had been convinced that the audience for base and tawdry stories was without limit. Just as the trial of Lorena Bobbitt had licensed them to use the dreaded word "penis" on the air, this affair had led to the first national debate about whether fellatio was the same as "sexual relations." Someone heard someone tell someone else that an Arkansas state trooper once said that Bill Clinton once said that it wasn't. Or perhaps it was Gennifer Flowers who said whatever was said. The double-talk was hilarious. Even Ted Koppel appeared unable to believe that he was actually saying what he was saying on the air.

Newspapers struggled to find ways to convey the language on the tapes made by that wonderful guardian of public morality, Linda Tripp. Posing as Ms. Lewinsky's dear and consoling friend, Tripp taped everything the younger woman was saying. The details did not resemble the novels of Jane Austen. One newspaper's solution was to run the phrase "b... j..," the first time in mainstream journalistic history that either "blow" or "job" had been placed on the obscene list. On one level, this was all raunchy fun, additional evidence that the cold war was over, that nothing at all meant anything at all. An example of cynical postmodern negation. Voices seemed to be saying, Hey, man, don't bother me with seriousness, okay? Get on the air. Get your minutes. Get on page one. Get the money. Nobody will remember a thing by tomorrow night.

But among most of the journalists I know there was a deepening sense of what can only be called shame. They didn't want to look at their own newspapers. They didn't want to bring them home and explain them to their children. They didn't want to be *in* them. It wasn't the essential grunginess of the story; it was the way it was being told, with eyes popping, tongues hanging out, and counterfeit emotions larding the writing.

"There's only gonna be one loser in this mess," one columnist told me. "Us."

The Lewinsky affair came at a time when most professionals believe that newspapers are in serious trouble. The competition from cable television and the Internet is no longer theoretical; it is very real. About 65 percent of the American people get their news from television, and the Internet is pulling at many people near the top of the newspaper circulation base in income and education. But increased competition for the attention of citizens is not the only reason for the problems of newspapers. In some cities, there have been self-inflicted wounds: bitter, often irrational strikes, abrupt changes in ownership, sluggish adjustments to new technology, failures to invest in modernization. Newspapers have also been hurt by the spiraling costs of newsprint; we will never again see a daily newspaper that sells for fifteen cents.

In addition, more newspapers are now in the hands of faceless chains or individual amateurs; both seem to believe that the abstract management techniques of other businesses—cereals, real estate, parking lots—can be applied without penalty to newspapers. Licensed by publishers, MBAs have been granted positions of power in many newsrooms. These men and women, who have never been reporters, depend upon polling and focus groups to shape the news package. They are responsible for the endless meetings, with their charts and abstractions, that consume so much time that was once used by editors to inspire and instruct the young and push the seasoned veterans to better stories. They slice and pare and trim in the name of the holy bottom line, extol the virtues of "reader-driven" journalism, and in the process witlessly reduce the possibilities for long-range growth.[1]

These are all important factors, but I believe one factor is more important than all others: content. With the usual honorable exceptions, newspapers are getting dumber. They are increasingly filled with sensation, rumor, press-agent flackery, and bloated trivialities at the expense of significant facts. The Lewinsky affair was just a magnified version of what has been going on for some time. Newspapers emphasize drama and conflict at the expense of analysis. They cover celebrities as if reporters were a bunch of waifs with their noses pressed enviously to the windows of the rich and famous. They are parochial, square, enslaved to the conventional pieties. The worst are becoming brainless printed junk food. All across the country, in large cities and small, even the better newspapers are predictable and boring. A movie director once said of a certain screenwriter: "He aspired to mediocrity, and he succeeded." Many newspapers are succeeding in the same way.

The most appalling thing about this decline in quality is that the people who make newspapers are aware of it. The trade weekly *Editor and Publisher* recently reported the results of a poll of the nation's publishers and editors.[2] Some 47.9 percent agreed that press coverage was "shallow and inadequate." About 55.7 percent thought coverage was too cynical. A huge 65.8 percent agreed that newspapers cover politics and personalities at the expense of policy. Those are the opinions of the *bosses*, the people who presumably can do something about the quality of the products they are selling. I'm certain that the opinions of the roughly fifty-six thousand men and women who work for the nation's 1,643 daily newspapers would be even more critical.[3] The most talented young writers, reporters, and photographers keep abandoning newspapers for other media. The industry's insultingly low salaries are only a minor reason. These craftsmen want to be proud of what they do for a living.

They want to work at the top of their talents, or to discover just how talented they really are. Most newspapers don't give them that chance. Newspaper people are notorious gripers, of course, but in the past decade I've heard more and more complaints about the cheapness, vulgarity, and mediocrity of newspapers from the people who work for them. One young woman, explaining why she was leaving a solid job at a newspaper for the hazards of freelancing, told me: "I don't want to keep apologizing for the place where I work."

The results of this wide perception of shrinking vitality are obvious. In many cities, newspapers have folded or merged with old rivals. Cities as varied as Los Angeles, Miami, New Orleans, Dallas, and San Antonio have become one-newspaper towns. Profits are up, because the economy, as I write, is in good shape and advertising revenues are rising. But almost everywhere, circulation is static or in decline, and too many readers buy a newspaper only twice a week.

One ominous index of the long-term problem is that from 1970 to 1990, the total weekday circulation of daily newspapers in the United States increased only 1 percent. It remains at about 60 million. During the same period, the country's population has risen more than 20 percent and the number of households more than 50 percent.[4] The opportunities are obvious; newspapers are not seizing those opportunities. To more and more Americans, newspapers are simply irrelevant. The old daily newspaper habit is eroding; for many, it isn't even forming. The dreadful performance in the early days of the Lewinsky affair only reaffirms the feeling of too many Americans: Newspapers don't really matter anymore.

When newspapers don't matter, they often die. When I was young in New York, before the triumph of television, there were seven city-wide newspapers, plus separate newspapers published in the Bronx, Brooklyn, and Queens. Today there are three, along with a small city edition of *Newsday*, the Long Island daily. On the subways, newspapers were once part of the dailiness of New York life, an essential part of the morning journey from home to work and the return journey in the evening. The newspapers published for the Bronx and Brooklyn were the first to vanish; then the afternoon papers were gone, destroyed by the expanded evening news on television. But for a long time, the newspaper habit persisted. Today, I seldom see people reading newspapers in the subway; if there are fifty people in a subway car, three will be reading one of the tabloids, the *Daily News* or the *New York Post*; one will study the *New York Times*; two will be reading a Spanish-language morning paper; three will be reading the Chinese broadsheets. Some riders will be absorbed in paperbacks (often of high quality) or computer printouts (among the young). The rest stare at nothing or doze.

In short, for those working people who use the subway, the newspaper habit has been broken. Yes: New

York, with its 3.6 million subway rides each day, is not a typical American city. New Yorkers are the only Americans who can choose among three daily newspapers. But the old vital relationship between newspaper and subway rider, driven by the sense that you weren't truly living in New York if you didn't read a newspaper, is gone.

I can't speak for every American city about anything, including their newspapers; nobody can. There are too many newspapers, too many variations in region and culture. But when I move around the country, I do notice the way people engage with newspapers, and everywhere I see variations of the same disconnection that I see in New York. I'm on a bus going from one end of Phoenix to another; nobody at all is reading a newspaper. I'm in a coffee shop in La Jolla; there are a few people reading newspapers, but I certainly hear no passionate debates under way about what they are reading. To be sure, in many cities, the bulk of a newspaper's circulation is home-delivered; there might indeed be intense focus on the content of the newspaper within the home. But somehow the experience of being in Chicago seems unfocused since the death of Mike Royko. San Francisco is certainly not the same since the death of Herb Caen. Big, swaggering voices and intensely passionate voices are giving way to bland, interchangeable voices that wouldn't frighten a rabbit. Almost all daily newspapers seem to resemble all other newspapers in the way they choose the news, the way they cover it, and the way they present it. Newspapers are more and more like television, where all local news shows resemble all other local news shows. I always think of this as area code 800 journalism. Nobody involved seems to be from a specific place; neither does the show or the newspaper.

This essay suggests some remedies for the present dilemma. It's a modest attempt to answer the question raised by many others, in a variety of fields: What is to be done? My take is personal, not neutral. But it is written with immense respect for the men and women who make newspapers. Those reporters, writers, photographers, and editors are the best Americans I know. They cherish the ideals of their imperfect profession and of the Republic whose freedoms, equally imperfect in practice, have so often made those ideals real. They want desperately to do good, honorable work. In spite of long hours and low pay, they are insistently professional.

They are also brave. I can't ever forget that in Indochina, sixty-five journalists were killed in the course of recording the truth about that war. They knew that only part of the truth could be discovered in the safe offices of Washington, D.C.; they had to witness the darker truths by getting down in the mud with the grunts. Reporters and photographers did not stop dying when Vietnam was over. They have been killed in Lebanon and Nicaragua, in Bosnia and Peru, and in a lot of other places where hard rain falls.

I can't believe that these good men and women died for nothing. I know they didn't. They died because they were the people chosen by the tribe to carry the torch to the back of the cave and tell the others what is there in the darkness. They died because they were serious about the craft they practiced. They died because they believed in the fundamental social need for what they did with a pen, a notebook, a typewriter, or a camera. They didn't die to increase profits for the stockholders. They didn't die to obtain an invitation to some White House dinner for a social-climbing publisher. They died for us.

As readers or journalists, we honor them when we remember that their dying was not part of a plan to make the world cheaper, baser, or dumber. They died to bring us the truth.

1

The Business and the Craft

A NY SYMPATHETIC EXAMINATION of newspapers must deal with several crucial matters. One is the craft of journalism and the way it is practiced. The other is the reality of the newspaper business as a business. They might sometimes be in conflict; they can't ever be separated. If a newspaper loses too much money over too long a time, it dies. Only a few newspapers—the *New York Post*, the *Washington Times*—have the luxury of ideologically driven subsidies that enable them to publish in the face of continued losses; the *Post* is published by Rupert Murdoch, the *Washington Times* by the Unification Church, and they share a conservative vision for America and the world. They are unique. No journalist can practice a craft for a newspaper that has gone out of existence. Every serious journalist knows this; most reporters, photographers, and editors want their newspapers to make money, so they can keep doing what they do. This is so obvious that it shouldn't have to be said.

Unfortunately, it is not so obvious to many of the businessmen who now call themselves publishers. Too many of them have a basic contempt for reporters; after all, they know how much money reporters earn, and in a world where money is used as a measure of value or accomplishment, they sneer at men and women who accept such comparatively menial wages. Worse, they often view reporters as a collective form of aggravating overhead; if they can eliminate enough jobs and still turn out a product that looks like a newspaper, they will do it. A publisher once told me: "Nothing beats the real estate business. You buy the land, you hire the architect, you build the building, you turn it over to an agent to manage. But you don't end up with a goddamned staff!" Another, a financial operator named Steve Hoffenberg, suggested that he could turn out the same newspaper, and a much more profitable one, if only he could fire all the reporters and hire a bunch of recent graduates of Ivy League schools. A third, parking lot entrepreneur Abe Hirschfeld, told me, "What do I need this aggravation for? Let me turn the building into a parking lot."

Such men are like the successful businessmen who buy baseball teams. Through buying their new business, they acquire instant celebrity. They appear on television and are profiled in magazines. They can get through on the telephone to the mayor, the governor, and, if the team is doing well enough, to the president of the United States. They are seldom humble. They believe that the skills that made them rich in other fields can be applied to baseball. After a very short while, they convince themselves that they are baseball experts, too. As such, they sit in harsh judgment of the baseball professionals, questioning plays, demanding explanations for inevitable losses. They have no true understanding of the game but revel in the power to humiliate those who do. Their teams almost always fail. They blame the managers. They blame the players. They never blame themselves. Such people never do.

Newspapers share certain other characteristics with sports franchises. They are capitalist entities that are also urban institutions, identified with specific cities. (The exception among newspapers is *USA Today*, and there is no sports equivalent, even though the Dallas Cowboys once claimed they were "America's Team.") The franchises have institutional histories, filled with heroes and goats, triumphs and failures, traditions that reach back through generations. Their fans have an often irrational sense of connection and identification with them that translates into loyalty and possessiveness. Such fans—the core audience—live in both the past and the present; they want nothing to change and everything to get better. They endure bad times, boring games, slumps, and failures because they have faith that things will get better. A pitcher will redeem a season with a no-hitter. An outfielder will hit four home runs in a single game. When the player excels, so does the fan. His or her identification with the team is then justified. Rooting for a specific team is like reading a specific newspaper: a badge of identity.

But the analogy is not exact; no sports analogy ever
is. Baseball, basketball, and football are part of the entertainment industry; newspapers are not, or shouldn't be.
Some newspaper stories can be presented in entertain-
ing ways; they can make you laugh; they can make you
weep. But they are not charged with providing exal-
tation or fantasy. In the most entertained nation in the
history of the world, newspapers exist to provide the citi-
zenry with truth. Sometimes the truth can have a moral
point. Sometimes the truth is painful. Sometimes the
truth is banal. But it *has* to be true. It must have a gran-
itelike foundation in fact. The mere stacking of facts is
not, of course, enough. The facts must be organized into
a coherent whole. They must tell a story. And the great
story usually tells us something larger than the mere facts,
something about what novelists and philosophers have
called, perhaps too grandly, the human condition.

Homer told us certain truths about the Trojan wars
and what they did to individual human beings; Homer
Bigart of the *New York Herald Tribune* and the *New York
Times* told us similar truths about wars in our own time.
The two Homers, thousands of years apart, were doing
the same work. They were adding to our knowledge and
understanding. In the end, newspapers must provide
both. We are part of the knowledge industry. We can't
be a mere diversion from the realities of the world; we
must help people to *understand* that world. Few of us are
presumptuous enough to believe that we are offering the

readers the gift of wisdom. But without knowledge, wisdom is impossible.

In the newspaper city rooms of America, there is never time for such discussion; if it came up at all, it would be scoffed at in a healthy way or dismissed as pretentious. But it is central to the enterprise. Every true journalist is trying to add to our knowledge. That is often at the heart of the conflict with the businessmen who have arrived late to the world of newspapers. The expansion of knowledge and the expansion of profits *can* be compatible; too often they are not.

Many publishers, corporate or individual, are more inclined now to meddle with the news side of the newspaper than at any time since the end of World War II. In some ways, they are throwbacks to the late nineteenth century and the first decades of this century, the era of Hearst and Pulitzer. They meddle most directly by haranguing top editors about stories, the play of those stories, and even writing style. They have never been reporters, have never written stories on deadline, have never stood for hours in the rain waiting for a detective to tell them what really happened. They know nothing about the city where the newspaper is published or the ordinary people who live in that city. But they are convinced they know more than the talent in the city room.

They can meddle indirectly, too, by tightening the budget screws, insisting on inflated profit margins. Those profits are seldom plowed back into the newspaper (as they have been for decades at the *New York Times* and other great newspapers). They are used to subsidize weaker members of a chain, to mollify shareholders (and ensure their own continued, richly rewarded employment), or to pay off large loans that made purchase of the newspaper possible. Occasionally, they have good intentions; too often, even good intentions are thwarted by arrogance. Or ignorance. Or both.

In most cases, these publishers are engaged in a process of chiseling away at the newspaper's ability to function, a process that also erodes staff morale. Sometimes the page size of the newspaper is trimmed, to save on newsprint. More often, the news hole—the amount of column inches devoted to news—is cut back. The reporters are forced to write shorter. This is not always a bad thing; some stories contain more bloat than significant detail or revealing context. But the usual result of such an order is a resigned superficiality. When reporters see their stories cut in half, day after day, with all grace notes excised, with any suggestions of complexity removed, they respond in two ways: they give up and send the editors what they want (instead of what the readers need), or they resign.

Obviously, the reduction of the news hole shrinks all coverage. If a newspaper still has foreign bureaus, which are expensive to maintain, they are the first to go. Foreign news is reduced to a stack of wire service briefs, unless there is a war or some other major calamity in which Americans are involved. Complicated investigative pieces also begin to fade off the schedules. They take too long to produce, are too expensive, and hey, do the readers really care? Television doesn't do this stuff anymore, so why should we? Editors sigh and cobble together replacements. Local features can be inflated by graphic designers to give the illusion of depth. This is cost-efficient: It takes the reader the same time to read stories of governmental skulduggery as it takes to read about lost dogs. Why bother?

The process acquires its own dynamic. The newspaper has three sports columnists? Get rid of one of them and make life miserable for another; maybe he'll resign. That features department: Get rid of most of them and buy canned features. Use the photograph from the movie company instead of sending your own photographer. Do one-shot interviews and don't bother with additional interviews that might give some roundness to the subject. You have your own editorial cartoonist, providing a local take on the events of the world? Can him and buy something from a syndicate.

In the end, of course, the readers wise up. They know that the reason their newspaper feels thin is because it *is* thin. The reason the newspaper feels flat and predictable is because it *is* flat and predictable. Less is not more. Less is less. When the publisher continues to charge fifty cents for a shrunken newspaper, the reader eventually understands that this is another case of consumer fraud; it is like reducing the size of a candy bar without reducing the price. Television news might be shrinking, too, but it doesn't cost the consumer fifty cents to tune in.

The remaining content and its presentation are also important to that reader. When screaming headlines turn out to be based on stories that don't support them, the tale of the boy who cried wolf gets new life. When the newspaper is filled with stupid features about celebrities at the expense of hard news, the reader feels patronized. In the process, the critical relationship of reader to newspaper is slowly undermined. True newspaper professionals have learned that the readers have immense common sense. The readers know that newspapers can't give them sensational, earthshaking news every day of the week because there isn't a sensational, earthshaking event happening every day of the week. If the headlines scream about the living arrangements of the sitcom actress Ellen DeGeneres, what will they do if there is another Hiroshima? In their own lives, ordinary readers have a sense of proportion: some events are more important than others. They don't expect a sensation every day. Steadiness, truthfulness, and reliability are crucial to the long-term relationship between newspaper and reader. Good newspapers are spouses, not lovers.

In the end, journalists know what too many modern publishers can't seem to admit: If newspapers are to flourish as *businesses*, they must make absolute commitments to quality as *newspapers*. American newspapers make their money from advertising. But if the readers don't believe the news stories in the newspapers, they won't believe the advertising. If readers feel that the content of the newspaper is superficial and sketchy, without much substance, they eventually will have similar feelings about the advertised products. If the newspaper treats the readers as if they are utter fools at worst and gullible airheads at best, then the advertisers will seem to be endorsing that attitude.

Those American newspapers with a continuing commitment to excellence—the *New York Times*, the *Los Angeles Times*, the *Washington Post*, the *Wall Street Journal*—are also healthy as businesses. The readers believe the news stories. They don't have to agree with everything in the newspaper or be completely happy with its coverage; they might not read every word of every story, since nobody ever does, not even editors. But they feel respected by the writers, columnists, and editors. They sense that the newspaper has made a genuine attempt to discover, within the limits of time and space, what was knowable about an event or a person in the news. They know that the newspaper tries to verify stories, to determine what is true and what is not. They know that their newspaper doesn't pander or attempt to inflame cheap emotions. Those readers don't expect perfection; they know that mistakes will be made and that they will be admitted in published corrections. They can quarrel with the newspaper, but it will be on an intelligent level. There is, between newspaper and reader, an element of trust. And the advertising in such newspapers is an endorsement of the journalistic attempt at excellence. If you can trust the news stories, you can trust the ads.

Those publishers who seek inspiration, or license, from the supermarket tabloids and try to publish less grungy versions of the tabloids' agendas are fools. Such weeklies have their own gaudy attractions, based on a sense of camp. They have a loony energy; they sometimes break solid stories; they can convey outrageous humor. But they are in the entertainment business, not the knowledge business. And they are not doing very well. Circulation was never very large in major cities; now it is eroding around the country. And they do not attract much advertising. Daily newspapers that try to emulate them, with a covering glaze of respectability, might get ads for gun permits, baldness cures, penile enlargements, phone sex, and strip joints. They will not get Bloomingdale's or Barnes & Noble or Compaq computers. And they will never grow.

2

Welcome to the
Zócalo

IN THE CITIES and towns of Mexico, the main plaza is
usually called the *zócalo*. It is a marvelous social institution. Along the sides of most such public squares are the
city hall, the central police station, and the church.
There is often a band shell in the center, surrounded by a
park, with benches under the trees and shoeshine boys
and newsdealers. Most buildings have arcades fronting
the square, and beneath the arcades there are cafés with
tables. In the evening, men and women of all classes ar-
rive from all districts of the town. Boys and girls walk in
groups, flirting, whispering. At the café tables, there is
much talk. At one table, the subject might be football. At
another, the cost of living. At a third, the perils of love.
Every sort of information is exchanged: news of politics, corruption, the cost of living. Each night, there are
thousands of small encounters, collisions, illuminations.
More important, there is a sense of *belonging* in the rude
democracy of the *zócalo*. The daily visitors belong to that

town. They are its citizens. They come to know its great men and strong women, its frauds and informers, its liars and its truth tellers, its solid citizens and its criminals. In the *zócalo*, they come to understand how the town works and who has real power. They understand clearly what factors—weather, devaluations, the larger economy—will affect their ability to put food on their tables. They go to the *zócalo* to learn.

The institution of the central plaza has never existed in the same way north of the Rio Grande. There is no unifying, centralizing plaza in New York or Chicago or Los Angeles. Our scale is too large, the cities too immense. Even our small-town equivalents—the town square or Main Street—have been abandoned for the glossier attractions of shopping malls. But I like to think of newspapers as psychological *zócalos*. A newspaper is a specific product; but it is also a common destination for citizens from all walks of life, a thing that is also a shared location. Those citizens might spend only a short time in the printed *zócalo*, but they can feel a small amount of comfort in the big, anonymous, alienating city in knowing that such a brief experience is common to hundreds of thousands of others.

The newspaper as plaza must be open to all those who want to learn more about the place in which they live and the world in which that place exists. If it is too narrow, too insistently rooted in the parish, it becomes by definition parochial. If its concerns are too ethereal, too remote from the lives of ordinary citizens, it will become a closed space, a kind of private club, a force for exclusion instead of inclusion. A newspaper must be open. It must communicate a sense of welcome. There is room in the *zócalo* for people who are interested only in sports or politics, crime or education. Some might want to know about changing fashions, the latest plays, movies, or music, the best restaurants. Some might want a laugh; they can turn to the comic strips. Some might want to hear the latest gossip.

"What is your audience?" is the question often asked of newspaper executives.

The answer should be a variation of: "Everyone in the *zócalo*."

For a daily newspaper, there is never a *single* audience. Newspapers are not magazines. Most national magazines are edited for a class or for a carefully defined group: computer freaks, fashion-conscious men or women, yacht owners, exercise and diet nuts, sports fans, and so on. Many of the old mass-circulation weekly magazines— *Life, Look, Collier's*, the *Saturday Evening Post*—were destroyed be television as completely as were afternoon newspapers. They were national magazines, attempting to serve broad audiences from Maine to Los Angeles; television did that much more effectively and powerfully.

But daily newspapers must be edited for a *community*, that is, for a specific city. Within that city, there are a variety of smaller audiences, with narrower needs and concerns. Those smaller groups must know that they will find what they need in the newspaper, while simultaneously discovering other matters of significant interest. If enough of these smaller groups get in the newspaper habit, they become part of that critical mass known as the readership. Publishers today know nothing about these people; publishers are rich and know many rich people, but you can't build a large newspaper readership composed of the rich. There will never be enough of them. The job of getting to know the people must fall upon the editors.

Editors have to think much harder about those fractional audiences. Since all cities are dynamic, the potential new audiences are always changing. One generation dies, another arrives; one ethnic group is assimilated, another shows up, raw and green. A newspaper that doesn't change as the city changes is certain to wither, even to die. There are a variety of ways for editors to discover what those potential new readers want on a daily basis. The pseudo-scientific techniques of polls and focus groups have their uses, but they aren't nearly good enough. Even if they were born in the city, newspaper editors have to work much harder at learning about the overlapping communities they are trying to serve. They have to know the city intimately, study its history, understand its cycles and rhythms, its language and myths, its legends and lore. Without such knowledge they can't ensure that the news has context. They can't instruct the young, push them, cajole them, inspire them to find stories and tell those stories with power and relevance.

Most of all, editors must learn by osmosis, by having daily lives among their readers. One of the saddest truths about today's newspapers is that too many of their editors live in the suburbs, sometimes the distant suburbs. One editor of an important western newspaper travels almost fifty miles each way to sit at his desk. In many cities the average young reporter, with limited experience and even more limited financial resources, knows more about the city than the top editors. The young reporter lives in the city, usually in a lower-class neighborhood, doubled or tripled up with other young people. The editors live in upper-middle-class security, far from reporters and readers.

There is a remedy for this absurd situation. Publishers should require in their contracts that all top editors must live in the city; if they want to live in the suburbs, they can find jobs editing suburban newspapers. To edit a newspaper in a major city is a great honor and a huge responsibility; refusing to live in that city is like a mayor deciding he will live in a town other than the one he governs. Editors must visit the *zócalo* every day of their lives. They should shop in their city and place their kids in that city's public schools. They should pay taxes in the city. Instead of collapsing in exhaustion before a TV set in the dubious comforts of the suburbs, they should dine in its restaurants, seek entertainment in the city's theaters, movie houses, and concert halls. They should use public transportation to move around the city (taxis are often necessary, of course, but they should never *ever* use limousines). In the 1920s and 1930s, when Joseph Medill Patterson was building the *New York Daily News* into the largest-circulation newspaper in the United States, he took subways every day. He watched the way citizens read his newspaper. If enough of them skimmed a feature, he took serious notice. If too many of them flipped past a comic strip, he called in the cartoonist for a critique or canceled the strip. The people of the city were his focus group.

When an editor comes to the city from the suburbs each morning by car or train, works many wearying hours, then repeats the same boring journey home, that editor is losing touch with the audience. He knows about the city from his reporters (if he has the rare common sense to trust their knowledge over his own). He hears about it on the car radio. He looks at the frequently inane city coverage on local television. But he is not really *experiencing* that city. He doesn't even have time to read about it. Eventually he and the newspaper will pay a price for this huge sin of omission.

Part of that price is the failure to recognize change. Changes in social attitudes. Changes in ethnic composition. Changes in the way men and women work for a living, or dress, or fall in love. Driving out of town on a freeway, it's hard to see the poor huddled in their roachy tenements. It's impossible to see *anybody* close up, one at a time. You can't hear the rise and fall of argument and contention. You don't see peril down the dark streets. You don't hear the music or the jokes. You seldom witness the major losses and the minor triumphs. The city becomes a blur. And in the blur, where news reports are always received secondhand from other people, it's difficult to recognize the big defining stories.

Some would remind me that certain major cities—Los Angeles, Phoenix, Atlanta—are really only vast, sprawling suburbs. I'm not sure that's true. I've wandered on foot through urban neighborhoods in Atlanta, stopped in blues joints, shopped in stores that were not parts of malls. When I'm in Los Angeles, I always go to East L.A., which is a true neighborhood, with middle-class folks in their own homes a few blocks from housing projects, dozens of shops, great music stores, fine restaurants, and a big main street that until recently was called Brooklyn Avenue. The Irish used to live there, and then the Jews, and now the Mexicans and their American children. The visitor sees more life in one block of Boyle Heights than in all of Brentwood. Even in Phoenix, there are dense neighborhoods near the university, thick with shops, restaurants, bookstores. None resemble the older eastern cities. They are horizontal cities, unrestricted by geography, built after the coming of the automobile; they had no need to emulate the verticality of the East. But they are cities nevertheless. Editors should know every block, be able to distinguish one neighborhood from another without asking, and discover their stories through contact, not surveys and focus groups. Living in the center of their dailiness is the only real way to do that.

To be separated from the readership by class *and* geography leads to two kinds of missed opportunities. One
is journalistic: the failure to see the best stories. The
other is for business growth. The opportunity for growth
exists today among two huge groups of human beings.
One of them is women. They're in the *zócalo*, all right,
but they can't find a table.

3

What Do Women Want?

EVERY NEWSPAPER WANTS more women readers. The reason is simple. Advertisers are convinced that married women make most of the consumer decisions in American families. They decide to buy the new toasters, the sets of dishes, the furniture and the food; they choose the clothing for themselves and their children and have a major say in how their husbands dress; they decide when a child is ready for his or her first computer. Men might choose the automobiles (which is why so many car ads run in the sports section), but in most families, women purchase everything else. In addition, there is a huge market among single working women. They buy clothes, shoes, makeup, and accessories for themselves. They buy books. They use travel agencies for vacations. They choose among any number of health clubs. They use services that range from special educational classes to home-delivered food. On dates, they usually choose the movie.

"If all the men in New York died of heart attacks to-morrow morning," an advertising man once told me, "and all the women survived, I'd still advertise in your newspaper."

Goods and services purchased by women are still most effectively advertised through newspapers; the old saw "You can't tear an ad out of a TV screen" is true. Department stores, whose institutional histories so closely parallel those of newspapers, must attract women customers or they will perish. They too have had to face intense competition from more narrowly focused stores; they have had to cope with rising overhead and the lower prices available to chains. Those that could not compete effectively for the business of women have died. If newspapers don't attract more women readers, they too will perish.

This has led to sporadic, occasionally panicky debate among newspaper editors, male and female. Much legitimate feminist scorn has been heaped upon the old "women's sections," with their tight focus on food and fashion, sketchy reporting, banal or breathless writing. Those sections were directed at women who had much leisure time. By the late 1960s, they were anachronisms. The modern American woman is often engaged in an exhausting juggling act. Most married women now work, full time or part time; they must find room for husband and family, bosses and jobs, while struggling for some moments of plain human privacy. Single women are engaged in a similar tug-of-war, pulled in separate ways by the demands of their professional lives and their own desire for private lives, working into the hierarchies of corporations while establishing homes for themselves. Single or married, the details are different but the conflicts are the same.

Many newspapers have attempted to renovate the old-fashioned women's sections to reflect these new realities. Some have done a superb job. In the 1970s, the Style section of the *Washington Post* and the Home section of the *New York Times* showed new ways to address the old content while broadening the range of subjects of their scrutiny. In general, both sections (which are otherwise very different) featured harder reporting, sharper writing, better photography, and more handsome graphics. They attracted readers and advertising; their principles have been widely imitated.

Another fine example of modernizing is the Thersday section of the *New York Daily News*. Created in March 1995 by a young Irish journalist named Orla Healy, this weekly seven-page section blends often sassy stories about clothes, "lifestyles" (that horrendous phrase), and consumer goods. The jazzy layouts are innovative and surprising without destroying readability. But the key to the success of the section is its consciousness of the specific audience: women who work.

One example of that vision: For the section's fashion shoots, Healy didn't use professional models. Instead she employed "real-world" people. These men, women, and children had the bodies and faces of human beings. They were not those ethereal, anorexic creatures that have never been spotted on the A train. They reflected the ethnic and racial diversity of the city. They looked like citizens of New York because they *were* citizens of New York. But from the beginning, her section was also absolutely practical, a superb example of "news you can use." Every story included hard information about price, because for most working women (married or single), high-fashion designer clothing is simply not practical; it is clothing for the rich. Every story in Healy's section contained exact prices and the names and locations of stores where those goods could be found. One of the implied points of the fashion coverage in Thursday was that working women—readers of the *Daily News*—could dress as smartly, even elegantly, as any reader of the *New York Times*. And could also afford it.

For many editors, one of the surprising things about these sections is the number of men who read them. When I was at the *Daily News*, Thursday provoked as many letters and calls from men as from women, some of them outraged, some of them full of praise. Men read the sections in a different way, of course: primarily to discover what women are thinking (run a story about the female orgasm and men *always* read it, too), but sometimes for more casual reasons: to have something to talk about on dates, for hints about gifts for women or kids. The reasons are varied. But these sections *are* read by men. They aren't ghettos for women readers. Such a goal would be absurd, because there are more women than men in the population and they can't be ghettoized.

That's why, in the end, the success of these sections can't be measured by the amount of advertising that runs in the specific sections. The sections must be part of a larger strategy to attract women readers to the *entire* newspaper. If they don't do that, they fail.

The urgent task of all newspaper editors is to make the whole paper essential and meaningful to more women. There are a number of ways to accomplish that goal. One of the most important is the involvement of professional women journalists at all levels of the editorial process. They must be among the top editors at every newspaper, and not as tokens; they must share the power to decide what stories are covered and how they are played. Newspapers are not, of course, democracies; if there is too much debate, too many endless meetings, the newspaper will never get out. But if the strategy is clear, and solid female professionals are added to the decision-making process, debate can be held to a minimum.

I don't mean to suggest here that women have been excluded from newspapers; clearly, they haven't. They are working on most beats, from city hall to the police shack. They cover wars and the White House, state capitols and the stock market. Many of the bravest, most accomplished photographers are women. At this point in our history, reporting is no longer an all-male macho club.

But on two levels, newspapers are simply not taking

advantage of the presence of so many talented women on their staffs. They don't *systematically* reach out to newspaperwomen themselves for advice about connecting with the larger female audience. Those reporters, copy editors, photographers, and designers didn't cease being women when they were given press cards. They should be part of the continuing process of making the newspaper more aware of what women want in its pages. They should critique the newspaper. They should be encouraged to write critical memos to editors without worrying about provoking thin-skinned responses. And then their opinions should be respected in the best possible way: by being put into effect.

The other failure is more about promotion than it is about journalism. Newspapers do a pathetic job of telling the potential audience about the women on their staffs. Every newspaper should promote its stars, regardless of gender: the columnists and prizewinners. It should never spend a dime on promoting the publisher, about whom the general public doesn't give a rat's ass. But if it takes a village to raise a child, it takes an entire staff to make a newspaper. Many members of newspaper staffs are now women who are indispensable to the process. There should be billboards, TV spots, radio commercials, and house ads that brag about the women who participate in the hard, grinding work of putting out the newspaper. Newspapers should explain what such women do, present them as role models for girls, and educate young men along with young women.

Television, the great competitor of newspapers, makes its women highly visible. The whole country knows Diane Sawyer, Katie Couric, Jane Pauley, Lesley Stahl, and Christiane Amanpour, to mention only some national stars. That visibility is largely due to the nature of the television medium; through nightly exposure, the young woman who reports on the weather is better known to the public than the average woman Pulitzer Prize winner. But networks and local stations aren't content with letting it go at that. They have budgets for promotional spots. They encourage profiles. They spend money to make their big names even more famous. Newspapers should do the same. They can go one step beyond television by showing that newspapers are produced by women who are not as famous but just as accomplished as the big names. That is, newspapers are made, in part, by women very much like the women who *buy* newspapers: smart, tenacious, brave, skilled, full of humor and irony. Newspaperwomen, unlike their television counterparts, share one other quality with their audience: They are dreadfully underpaid.

In the end, of course, newspapers must be judged by the stories that appear on their pages and how they are presented, that is, by their substance and style. In polls, focus groups, and private conversations, women have made clear that they care deeply, even passionately, about certain issues. Most important of all is education. Parents want to know why their children are falling behind or failing. They want to know if teachers are qualified and committed to their task. They want to know if the schools are safe from hoodlums or tottering because of shoddy construction and maintenance. They want to know what percentage of the city's budget is devoted to schools and how that money is spent. They have a healthy skepticism about press releases from the board of education or speeches by politicians. They want hard, verified information about the theory and practice of education. It is not easy for reporters to cover practice *and* policy while in the company of a camera crew; video cameras themselves alter the behavior of children and teachers. The best medium for conveying information about education is the newspaper.

In most polls, education is usually followed by a need for information about the environment. For men and women who live in cities, this doesn't mean reports from the Sierra Club about the fate of the spotted owl. Women want to know if the tap water is safe. They want to know if their children are more likely to develop asthma in certain areas of the city. They want to know if chemical plants across the river are filling the lungs of their children with carcinogens. They want assurances that someone is inspecting the meat and fish they are buying in the market.

They also want solid information about health. Not just disease, but prevention. That includes diet and exercise. Too often, stories about fad diets are run without solid reporting; it should be the obligation of every newspaper to examine fad diets and best-selling diet books, consulting with reputable nutritionists and those government agencies charged with policing the country's health. Millions of Americans, most of them women, were lured into the use of fen-phen to lose weight; it wasn't until the *New York Daily News* published alarming reports about its hazards that the government stepped in and the fad was ended. That's what newspapers do best: reveal dangers and provoke action.

It would be foolish to think that women don't care about the rest of the newspaper. Before they are women, they are residents and taxpayers of an American city. Those who serve as heads of households—married or single—want solid information about the state of the economy and how it will affect their lives. If criminals are roaming the streets of their neighborhoods with impunity, or selling drugs, they want newspapers to hear their cries for help, so that an indifferent police force will be compelled to act. They walk those streets. Their children play in those streets. They have only marginal interest in the latest sensational sex scandal; they do care when death comes calling in their own neighborhood.

They care about other things, too. Taxes. Inefficient government bureaucracies. The endless capacity of the human race for folly, which is the source of most laughter. Women are not grim, tightly focused creatures; they want some laughs, too. But they also want context. As citizens, they are just like men: They need hard information if they are to think intelligently about what James Joyce once called "those big words . . . which make us so unhappy." They want to know what the people in Washington are doing, and they want to find out by reading coherent stories based in fact. Like most Americans, they have little interest in the wretched little games inside the Beltway. But they know that politicians can cause much grief in the name of airy abstractions, all those big words. They know that if the country starts drifting into another war, politicians won't fight in that war; their own children will.

Obviously, as adolescents become young women, there are ongoing stories that require continuous examination and updating by newspapers. One is abortion. Since women could be directly affected by the politics of abortion, they should have solid information about the players in that endless debate, the financing of the pressure groups on both sides of the argument, and the way these groups might affect politicians through campaign contributions. They should have absolutely accurate accounts of the health issues involved, based on medical facts, not political or moral interpretations. The political and moral debate is certainly important and should be accurately reported. Its complexities can be given ample space on op-ed pages, where contributors should be given clear identifications. (Think tanks, left and right, usually adopt preposterously vague and pompous names to promote the illusion of detachment and neutrality; they should be characterized for what they are—liberal, conservative, anarchist, or vegetarian—to assist those readers who don't keep track of such arcane matters.)

Good editors should always keep one motto in mind: Just because a story has been published, it is not necessarily over.

There are other ways to make newspapers more vital to women. Women columnists have a place in all sections of the newspaper, including more than ever in sports. Millions of young women now play in organized sports; they understand the language of sports, the rules, the nuances. The subject provokes as much passion among women as among men. Over the past dozen years, I've had spirited, detailed discussions with women about almost every major sport. If, like men, they don't continue playing after school ends, they continue as fans. Sports fans usually know the score from television or radio, but they are absorbed by statistics, details, and what was said in the dressing rooms. The best medium for such material is the newspaper. The sports section can't be a closed shop for men; it must attract more women sports reporters, assign them to major sports, and make them visible to the readers. This is good journalism, but it also makes good business sense. One recent survey by the National Basketball Association revealed that 40 percent of basketball fans are women. When the Women's National Basketball Association put its New York team on the court at Madison Square Garden, the audience began filling up with women and young African-Americans. One reason: For the first time in years, these fans could actually afford to go to basketball games in the Garden.

Editors should consider one other matter when thinking about attracting more women readers: tone. In my experience, women don't like being shouted at. They don't like being patronized. They don't like being treated as if they were stupid. They don't like stories that present women as brainless bimbos. They don't like macho swagger in the men they meet or marry, in politicians, or in newspaper columnists.

Tone is a matter of style. All newspapers think about style, but for a long time they have been preoccupied by graphic style. Television forced newspapers to add color, to become more graphically handsome. Old newspapermen originally sneered at *USA Today* when it began publishing in 1982. It was "McPaper," a kind of McDonald's of newspapers. Or it was printed television. Diagrams and fact boxes seemed to overwhelm stories. Major stories were so compressed that they appeared to be sketchy and underreported. But several surprising things slowly happened: *USA Today* got better and better as a newspaper, featuring hefty, well-reported front-page stories, smart features, and thorough sports and entertainment coverage. At the same time, many newspapers, which originally sneered, began scrambling to adopt its graphic innovations.

Graphics and typography are essential to conveying a newspaper's tone. But so is writing style. So is the way certain kinds of news and features are presented. Graphics, writing, and news judgment are the basic components of a newspaper's tone. All three combine as a statement of what the editors think about the readers. If the front page screams about trivialities, the editors clearly believe that the readers respond only to hysterical bellowing. If it carries a daily dose of in-your-face blood-and-guts accounts of cheap murders, it says that the reader cares only about mayhem. If the front of the paper is crowded with half-baked celebrity stories while substantial news is trimmed to briefs and shoved in the back, the editors are saying, "You are all dumb bastards." Not many women feel comfortable in a cheap saloon.

In short, there are a number of ways to attract more women readers. And there are ways to repel them. If editors are determined to drive women away, they should patronize them. They should fill the paper with salacious gossip, so that women can't ever bring it home. They should treat women as if their heads are teeming with trivialities and gossip. Above all, they should shout at them.

But the next sound those editors will hear is Nora slamming her door.

4

Tell It to Abdul
(or Kim, or Ivan, or Rosa . . .)

I N 1922, WHEN the *New York Daily News* was three years old, its advertising department invented a slogan that swiftly became the newspaper's basic motto: "Tell it to Sweeney! The Stuyvesants will understand."

The message was simple. The Sweeneys were working-class New Yorkers, immigrants or their children; not all of them were Irish. The Stuyvesants were the uptown New Yorkers, more prosperous, owners of property, tracing their heritage back to old Dutch burghers or the WASP ascendancy. The *Daily News* was not telling the Stuyvesants to read another paper. They were saying that the paper was a big tent, with room for the Sweeneys *and* the Stuyvesants. And there were always more Sweeneys. If a newspaper was to be a mass medium, it had to get the Sweeneys as readers and then convince advertisers that they were a huge market.

The United States is now in the midst of the largest

immigration wave since the turn of the last century, and the arrival of so many strangers among us is both a challenge and an opportunity for newspapers. Not many of the new immigrants are named Sweeney anymore (although there are substantial numbers of Irish immigrants, legal and illegal, in some major cities). Instead of Italian and Yiddish, they speak Korean, Spanish, Russian, Hindi, or one of a hundred other languages. But they are here in search of the same things the European immigrants wanted: economic betterment for themselves and their children, personal and political freedom, and a measure of happiness. They don't come to America to feel worse.

Newspapers must cover this story in a sustained way for two reasons. First and most important is because the new immigrants are a great story. They are adding muscle to the workforce. They are changing neighborhoods and cities. They are providing social cement for certain "inner-city" neighborhoods, bringing new life to decayed buildings, creating small businesses, affirming the work ethic. They are altering the culture, producing novelists and poets along with musicians and actors and comedians. They are certainly improving the variety and quality of the food in our restaurants. In most cities, their crime rates are low, and not many find their way to welfare. Their energy can be infectious, too; they are showing many poor Americans that in the United States, personal history is less important than the willingness to work. Even the failures, the disappointments, the descent of a small number into crime or drugs are part of a much larger, marvelously positive narrative. Only newspapers run by fools would avoid covering this story.

The second reason for intelligent, positive coverage of immigration is practical: It is good business. If newspapers are reckless, careless, inadvertently racist in their present coverage, they will pay a price in the long run. Immigrants and their children have long memories. They remember how they were treated when they were poor and powerless, incorporating such treatment into the immigrant myth of overcoming obstacles. There are still some Irish-Americans who speak of the *Boston Globe* and the *New York Times* with contempt because of ancient slights printed in their pages. Some newspapers have residual reputations for being racist, anti-Semitic, or anti-union. I don't mean that newspapers should reduce their coverage of new immigrants to flag-waving chamber of commerce pap. But they must look at these new arrivals with respect and then provide an ongoing, well-reported context for their stories. Many newspapers have done series on the new immigrants that are well reported and usually respectful. But they can be only the *beginning* of coverage, a kind of overture. The coverage that follows the overture must be as sustained and steady as any other important beat. If immigrants and their children are to become regular readers of newspapers, they must feel that they are part of the city's unfolding story.

Many immigrants, of course, don't speak English; they do not become *immediate* readers of English-language newspapers. This is not new. The vast majority of Jewish and Italian immigrants didn't speak English, and neither did about 25 percent of the famine Irish, who arrived in the late 1840s. Newspapers can't expect large numbers of immediate readers from sustained immigrant coverage.

But if newspapers work hard and intelligently at the challenge, they will reap immense benefits. Even a cursory look at Spanish-language television illustrates the process that is already well under way. Every Spanish channel, morning and evening, runs commercials for English-language schools. The point of most of the commercials is clear: To be successful, to get a better-paying job and a better life, you must learn English. The existence of such schools, and the impulse that lies behind them, even offers a *short-term* opportunity for reaching this future audience. Newspapers are extraordinary teaching tools in the process of learning another language. When I was trying to learn Spanish as a GI Bill student in Mexico in the mid-1950s, I learned more about the language from the daily sports papers than I did from the grammar classes. I knew the basic thrust of most stories was that somebody won and somebody lost; there were Spanish words for *hit* and *run*, *first* and *home*; there were common and proper nouns and critical verbs. I needed a dictionary at first; soon I was reading, and speaking, without looking up the words. To be sure, my Spanish was imperfect, even comical. But it allowed me to buy food, get directions, count my change, and above all be polite.

Aggressive circulation managers should be in touch with every language school in a city, trying to make deals to introduce their newspapers from the beginning of the learning process. Offer steep discounts to the schools. Sponsor essay contests for the students, with prizes that include scholarships, encyclopedias, dictionaries, and free home delivery of the newspaper. Create study guides that teach newcomers how to read and use the morning newspaper. Nothing should be taken for granted. A few years ago, a new Chinese reader asked a *Daily News* editor, bashfully but with complete seriousness, how to read a baseball box score. This was a serious question. Baseball was a kind of Rosetta stone for immigrants such as my father; he learned more about being an American from baseball writer Dick Young of the *Daily News* than he ever did from reading about George Washington or studying Tocqueville. Some immigrants come from countries where baseball is a passion; others never heard of it. Its considerable mysteries should be explained.

In the effort to spread the presence of the newspaper and its educational role, every newspaper should create its own map of the city's demographics, detailing with the thoroughness of a war map where the newcomers live. The maps should show, block by block, where there are concentrations of Mexicans, Russians, Dominicans, Pakistanis, or other immigrants. They should locate newsstands, delicatessens, bodegas, and other locations where newspapers are, or can be, sold. This can't be done by computer. It can't be done by mail. It can't be done by combing the yellow pages. It must be done door-to-door. Generals depend upon intelligence gathered "on the ground"; they don't ever send soldiers into unknown territory.

Once basic intelligence is gathered, newspapers must act. Salespeople must go personally (not by telephone) to all these venues and persuade vendors to order their newspapers. They should provide sales materials—posters, stickers, T-shirts—that can help make the newspaper visible. But then they must keep track of what is happening after the orders are placed. Perhaps most important, they should be certain that their delivery trucks actually serve those communities in a *timely* way. This is no small matter. Most working people report to work at 8 A.M., not 10 A.M.; if a newspaper arrives at the bodega, deli, newsstand, subway, or bus stop after 7 A.M., that's too late. Newspapers have a shorter shelf life than milk. The greatest newspaper in the history of the planet cannot be sold to someone who has already left for work.

In the end, of course, content will be the determining factor in the effort to expand readership. Newspapers are not mere objects of paper and ink; they must tell us something new. Immigrants don't want to read only about themselves. They do care about immigration policy and how the maddeningly frequent changes in immigration laws and procedures can directly affect them. They care about the politics of immigration. They will always care if immigrants are being pushed around *because they're immigrants*. They want to believe that they're being treated in the same way as all other residents of the city, and are outraged when they are not.

But as newcomers, they want useful, relevant information about the city in which they are living. They want a scorecard that identifies the city's major players. They want to know about jobs, housing, schools, and crime. If the city described by the newspaper is too drastically different from the city of their personal experience, the paper won't be credible to them.

Obviously, to cover this new presence in American cities, editors must have the proper tools. One of the most important tools is language. The need for Spanish-speaking reporters has been obvious for years, and on the whole, it is being met. But in most big cities, there now must be staff reporters who speak Russian, Chinese, Korean, Hindi, or other languages, depending upon the size of immigrant groups. If there are no reporters available who speak those languages, then newspapers should pay for language training among existing staff members. This is being done at more newspapers now, and has been routine for decades when preparing reporters for foreign assignments. The process should be accelerated. As part of the process, editors could arrange for immigration reporters to spend periods of time at the newspapers of the immigrant communities, not simply to try out their language skills, but to develop contacts, sources of information, and generally better understand the subjects of their future journalistic scrutiny.

The presence of these foreign-born Americans underlines another colossal failure of all American media: foreign coverage. We keep hearing about the global economy. We keep seeing evidence that what happens in Thailand or Indonesia or South Korea can have consequences on Wall Street and then on Main Street. But television has virtually abandoned coverage of foreign affairs, unless there is a possibility of Americans dying. Newspapers are not much better. We cover the world the way we cover the Olympics: If no Americans are involved, we are not interested. With the usual exceptions, the foreign bureau is history, as dead as John Gunther, William L. Shirer, and Dorothy Thompson, who were stars in the great era of the foreign correspondent. Once-proud television news operations, like that of CBS, now buy film and videotape that wasn't shot by its own people; they often add voice-overs in the safety of their studios, remote from the action. Newspapers paste together networks of stringers, who are basically freelancers desperate to get into print in order to get paid, and therefore too vulnerable to the temptation to hype. Ask publishers about this and you hear the same weary refrain: "Americans just don't care about foreign news." To which the reply should be: "Which Americans?" Followed by: "How the hell do *you* know?"

In my experience, new Americans are passionately concerned about events in the countries they have left behind. They want to feel that their decision to emigrate was correct. They want to know what is happening to those who stayed home. Candidates for the presidency of the Dominican Republic now campaign in New York City; many immigrants send money home to encourage politicians they support. Immigrant newspapers now, like immigrant newspapers of a hundred years ago, are full of news about the old country—not weather reports, but reporting. Mainstream newspapers should think hard about this. It really isn't enough to use wire copy and briefs as a substitute for sustained foreign coverage geared to a specific audience. But at the very least, editors should focus their use of wire copy to take into account the presence of the new Americans. I don't mean that coverage of the Dominican Republic, Korea, Mexico, and Pakistan should replace the most important foreign stories of the day; but they must be *in* the newspaper. And whenever possible, editors should localize major foreign stories. If there is a political assassination in Mexico, a hurricane in the Dominican Republic, a fiercely contested election in Pakistan, or a financial collapse in South Korea, reporters should be sent to the immigrant neighborhoods. They can almost always find human reactions to what seem to be distant calamities. They can examine the way immigrants help afflicted people back in the old country with food, clothing, or money. They can understand political and social connections between their cities and distant places. This is not simple market-driven journalism; it is a journalism of *connection*, making the remote seem more local and therefore more human.

Obviously, editors can't sit back passively and wait

for the huge story of the new Americans to unfold. Like most good stories, it is not the subject of press conferences or photo opportunities, except during election years. This is a story that can be discovered only through reporting. Editors can't learn about the new immigrants while playing golf with bankers. They won't learn much about them in the suburbs, where the only Spanish-speaking people they are likely to meet are nannies or men mowing the lawns or cleaning the swimming pools. They won't find out much about anything at all while wedged in their offices. They have to go out themselves, or trust the people who do.

Editors can start by making personal connections with the foreign-language press in their own cities. Weeklies and dailies catering to immigrants are proliferating in large American cities. They are finding audiences. Editors of mainstream newspapers should get to know the editors of those immigrant newspapers, meet with them on a regular basis, open the doors of their own newspapers to show them how modern technology and printing systems work, treat them as colleagues. If they are treated with proper respect, those immigrant editors will become part of an early warning system for mainstream editors, making them aware of major controversies, shifts, trends, and problems among the new immigrants.

There are other ways of reaching out that also allow the children and grandchildren of earlier immigrant waves to recognize that in most essentials, the newcomers are in the great American tradition. First, editors should know what they are talking about. They should study the history of immigration and focus on the role played by the immigrant European press from the 1840s all the way to the 1930s. Any big-city editor, for example, who knows nothing about Abraham Cahan and the *Jewish Daily Forward* is an ignorant fool.

Then editors must get specific. They can start designing features that are informative for all readers but of special interest to newcomers. Sometimes this is a simple case of modernizing old ideas. For years, the "then and now" feature was a very popular staple of newspapers; a fifty-year-old photograph of a certain street corner and a new photograph of the same corner would show the great changes that had taken place. That feature can be reinvigorated, given new relevance with additional information. Who lived on that street fifty years ago? The Irish? The Jews? The Italians? And who lives there now? Dominicans? Mexicans? Koreans? How did the first wave of immigrants make out in America? Were there men and women of great accomplishment raised on those streets? When and why did the changes begin to happen? And in what generation? If such information is not in the clips, because the newspaper did a wretched job fifty or seventy-five years earlier, the facts can now be traced through the Internet, or by calling on the specialized knowledge of urban historians or sociologists. These stories always have great appeal to readers. For older citizens, they evoke nostalgia; for the newcomers, surprise; for both, a sense of continuity in the presence of change.

There are other ways of informing both older readers and potential new ones about the cities they now share. Every newspaper should make the attempt to go back to its own history and tell the tale. Howard Kleinberg of the *Miami Herald* does a fine job of this, making history seem fresh and relevant to the present. We should remember that the new immigrants have an idea of America but not a lot of facts. And the history of a particular city is almost never taught in the local school system. Newspapers can tell that tale. Ezra Pound was a great poet and a political fool, but he once had a useful definition for literature. He called it "news that stays news." That definition could also apply to history. When I was a boy, the *Brooklyn Eagle* ran a series of articles on the history of various communities in the borough. I was eleven years old and I devoured them. I kept announcing to my friends on the street: "Hey! George Washington retreated down Third Street when he lost the Battle of Long Island!" Or "Wow, they buried Dutchmen right down Flatbush Avenue!" The stories made the city come alive, they made history more vivid, they made me feel part of the long narrative. The articles were later reprinted as pamphlets. A half-century later, I still own my set.

There are other features that could help create two-way connections. At the *Daily News*, we started a weekly page of excerpts from the immigrant press. We ran small cuts of the front pages of these newspapers. Staff members and freelancers translated foreign-language pieces, but we also had excerpts from Irish weeklies, from the Indian press, and from papers representing the English-speaking Caribbean community. There were several benefits to this weekly page. The editors of those newspapers were pleased to have attention paid to their efforts and bragged about it in their own newspapers. That helped readers know about the *Daily News*, sending a message to the immigrants themselves that their concerns were also of interest to us. And the immigrant newspapers themselves became a useful source of stories for the city desk of the *Daily News*.

Unfortunately, publishers are not always willing to spend the money to make this effort. If a story doesn't sell papers tomorrow, they have no interest; long-range investments seem beyond their imagination. I've heard publishers sneer at the commercial potential of the new immigrants. The immigrants don't read. Or they can't read. Or advertisers aren't interested in them. Why waste space on this kind of coverage when we can run the tenth or even twentieth reprise of the death of Princess Di?

The men who built the great popular newspapers didn't have that attitude. Joseph Pulitzer, for example, didn't scoff at immigrants. He was himself an immigrant from Hungary, the son of a Catholic mother and Jewish father. He arrived in the United States in 1864, barely speaking English, and served as a teenage soldier in the

Civil War. After the war he found a job in St. Louis at a German-language weekly called the *Westliche Post* and started on the road to becoming one of the giants of American journalism. At thirty-one, he bought a newspaper called the *Dispatch*, soon merged it with the *Post*, and created the *St. Louis Post-Dispatch*. He built it into a powerhouse. But he was even more successful with the *New York World*, which he took over in 1883. The newspaper was losing money when he bought it from financier Jay Gould. But he had ideas, empathy, passion, and one great historical piece of good luck: the enormous tide of European immigration flowing into New York. They came with almost nothing except hope. And Pulitzer wanted them.

He understood that in publishing, quality is also good business. He swiftly made his newspaper a huge popular success with a simple formula: crusading investigations, tough reporting, clear and lively writing, and popular features that helped educate the readers. When he took over the newspaper, he made his populist intentions clear to his editors: "Heretofore you have all been living in the parlour and taking baths every day. Now I wish you to understand that, in the future, you are all walking down the Bowery."[1] Some of them resigned that day. Pulitzer himself walked among the poor of the Bowery, and his anger drove the newspaper to success. He was furious with the working and living conditions of immigrants, who were arriving at the rate of a thousand a day. He was no socialist, but he had his reporters emphasize the great differences between the lives of the wealthy and the lives of the immigrant poor. He didn't sneer at immigrants who spoke no English; on his arrival he had known little English himself, and if he could learn, so could they. The *New York World* would help educate them.

As his biographer W. A. Swanberg would later write:

> Pulitzer was the first to exploit, to publicize, to attack the shameful incongruity between Murray Hill and the Lower East Side and to demand corrective social and political action. He was indeed the first of the muckrakers. The *World* regularly assailed the "low upper classes," the "vulgar wealthy," the "watered stock aristocracy." It welcomed the immigrants who "bring us strong blood and unlimited possibilities." It courted the Irish by devotion to Home Rule and scorn for the English, the Germans by news of Bismarck and of Liederkranz balls, the Jews by attention to Purim. It aided them with incessant skillful crusades against their greatest enemies—corruption, complacency, the robber-baron mentality, a wage scale insuring serfdom, a reprehensible tax system, and appalling housing and health standards.[2]

Pulitzer's newspaper was never somber. It ran entertainment features and gossip. It gave great attention to crime and murder trials. The writing was simple, brisk, vivid. Throughout his career, Pulitzer insisted on the use of illustration and graphics and encouraged the use of news and feature photography. He experimented with gravure and color. He invented the comic strip by publishing R. F. Outcault's *Hogan's Alley*, featuring the Yellow Kid. He led the fight to raise money to place the Statue of Liberty in New York Harbor, thus creating the most enduring symbol of the American immigrant myth.

"One measure of the *World*'s greatness," Swanberg wrote, "was its insistence on treating the poor as human beings rather than ciphers."[3]

That empathy with the poor was one of the engines of another great populist newspaper: the *New York Daily News*, founded in 1919 by Joseph Mcdill Patterson. He was a remarkable man. Born rich, a grandson of the founder of the *Chicago Tribune*, Patterson was a former socialist who had managed the 1908 presidential campaign of Eugene V. Debs. He was the author of two proletarian novels and three Broadway plays, and he served as a war correspondent in Mexico, Europe, and China. In London during World War I, he was impressed by Lord Northcliffe's tabloid *Daily Mirror*. He thought New York, a subway town where broadsheets were difficult to read in crowded rush-hour trains, would embrace a tabloid. He was right.

Patterson respected working people and saw them as crucial to his new morning paper. The great immigrant tide was now over, halted by World War I and restrictive quotas. But the immigrants and their children made up the bulk of the city's population. Like Pulitzer almost forty years earlier, Patterson wanted them. He made that mission clear to the men he chose to run the newspaper, and they would eventually build it into the largest circulation newspaper in the United States.[4]

The "Tell it to Sweeney!" campaign wasn't an empty sentiment or a veiled declaration of the class struggle. It was supported by one of the earliest examples of intelligent market research. In 1922, a young woman named Sinclair Dakin was assigned by the newspaper's advertising director, Leo McGivena, to investigate the Lower East Side, then (and for years after) the epitome of a New York slum. Big advertisers were convinced that the poor immigrants and shop girls who were buying the *Daily News* just weren't worth luring to their stores. They were too poor. Dakin was asked to find out what these poor people bought, and why, and how much they spent.

The results were surprising, and in many respects, they are as true now as they were then. After slogging, door-to-door reporting, Dakin wrote:

The East Side today is not the East Side of twenty years ago, or even ten years back. The swollen immigrant stream of previous decades has shrunk to the thin trickle of the quota. High wages and the desire for better living conditions have swung the one-time immigrant upward to the crest of new purchasing power.

The East Side is a rich market—concentrated, accessible, appreciative, progressive. Many alert advertisers, such as Bordens, Huyler's, Babbitt's, White Rose Tea, Royal Baking Powder, Corn Products Refining Company and scores of distributors have already recognized its capacity and sell millions of dollars of goods annually in this tiny territory of one and three-fourths square miles.

In many respects the East Side is an *excess* market, because the East Sider has more margin between his income and essential cost of living than anybody else in New York. His surroundings, associates, and social status spare him many of the expenses the rest of us take for granted and unthinkingly assume. Consequently, he can splurge in many directions and the native born cannot.[5]

This was an extraordinary discovery. The uptown crowd was so loaded down with social obligations, high rents, expensive clothes, private schools, and servants that the poor of the Lower East Side actually had a larger percentage of spendable income. They bought food (and recognized brand names before they could say them), clothes, shoes, hats, baby carriages, cars, and more Russian caviar than any other New York neighborhood. In that small area, there were more than forty banks and trust companies. And although half the area's residents were foreign-born (primarily Eastern European Jews, but with large numbers of Italians and Chinese, and clusters of Greeks, Poles, Germans, and Irish), they were working hard at becoming Americans.

"The career of the newly arrived immigrant becomes, immediately on his arrival, a constant assimilation of American ideas, desires and buying habits," she wrote in her marketing report. "At first, the American habit of receiving information from the printed page may be strange to him. But on the East Side word of mouth travels like the wind! And the intelligent and progressive strive to read as well as speak the English or American language. The ability to read an American newspaper is often a prerequisite to citizenship papers, and a social step up."[6]

Based on this research, which he made available to all potential advertisers, McGivena wrote his "Tell It To Sweeney!" ads for the trade press. One key paragraph:

> You men who aspire to sell large bills of goods in New York, remember the Sweeneys. They comprise 75 percent of any large city's population. Address your advertising, your sales messages to them, because they are your best customers. They keep right on living and dying, earning and spending money, buying and using merchandise.

They are not hard to sell, and they *are* good folks
to do business with. And remember, when you
talk to Sweeney, the people of bluer blood and
more money who read *The News* will understand; whereas if you talk to Stuyvesants, the
Sweeneys won't listen. You can't lose by saying
it so Sweeney understands.[7]

This helped define the style and mission of the young
Daily News, and its success was picked up by many other
newspapers in the decades that followed. The writing
was clear, strong, and irreverent. The headlines were
witty. The subject matter was raffish, ranging from society divorces to Hollywood scandals, the doings of gang-
sters to the adventures of rogues. The sports section was
tight and well written, with brilliant action photographs.
In the *Daily News*, Patterson carried out the logic of
Pulitzer's innovations, mixing news, sports, and features
with flat-out entertainment. He developed the best comic
strips in America, from Milton Caniff's elegant and sexy
Terry and the Pirates to the slapstick rowdiness of Frank
Willard's *Moon Mullins*, from the brutally tough *Dick
Tracy*, jammed with Chester Gould's amazing villains, to
Frank King's wonderful Americana saga, *Gasoline Alley*.
Sydney Smith's *The Gumps* and Harold Gray's *Little Or-
phan Annie*, along with all the other comics, had a pur-
pose. They weren't in the newspaper to attract new
readers so much as to hold on to the ones who already

bought the paper. They were part of Patterson's larger plan to establish habit, loyalty, and continuity among *Daily News* readers. His success was astonishing.

Patterson would be appalled by today's ghettoized comics pages, so crammed with strips and panels that they look like stamp collections. Patterson ran fewer strips than some other newspapers, but that allowed him to give his strips good play. He wanted the comics to be read with as much concentration as sports or news, and he spent money to make them look good. Milton Caniff once told me that his beautiful four-color *Terry* Sunday pages were the responsibility of a single old German engraver.

In the pages of the *Daily News*, Patterson published popular fiction, too, in the form of short stories or brief serials. He ran advice to the lovelorn and health columns, etiquette panels, and crossword puzzles. His promotion people invented many contests to attract readers. He sponsored the Golden Gloves for male readers and the Harvest Moon Ball dance contests for women. But he knew that the vitality of the news side of the paper was basic to growth. He hired the best photographers in New York and added a tag to the masthead: "New York's Picture Newspaper," with a stylized Speed Graphic camera as the logo. He paid his reporters and writers better than any paper in town and was the first New York publisher to sign a contract with the Newspaper Guild. One reason for this action (it outraged his fellow publishers) was probably some residual loyalty to the ideals of his youth; another was common sense. New York was, and is, a union town. A publisher can't long survive if he sees his readers as the enemy.

Patterson, in fact, had an insatiable curiosity about his readers. He would take the subway to Coney Island and hang around bars and dance halls. He would prowl speakeasies and Broadway joints. He would visit Brooklyn and Queens and the Bronx, often on his own. He chatted with boilermakers and secretaries, longshoremen and department store clerks, cops and firemen. He was shy in many respects, not comfortable at parties or in the company of café society. But he loved wandering the city. He seemed to love its people.

Some of the methods of Pulitzer and Patterson are no longer viable. They couldn't be. Cities change, and newspapers must change with them. Pulitzer was in his heyday before radio and motion pictures permanently altered so much of the world and the city and the way we live in both. Patterson built his powerful tabloid before the advent of television. Newspapers are creatures of their own time, and this is the time of television. Newspapers can no longer compete with television on breaking news. Certain older features—narrative comic strips, short fiction—have also been supplanted by the pulp fiction and sitcoms that dominate television entertainment. The huge newspaper circulations of the past might never be seen again (although I believe they can be much larger). But if newspapers don't service the city that *is*—instead of the city that *was*—they will just keel over and die.

Because the circumstances are different, the approach to attracting immigrant readers must be different. The European immigrants had to learn English to be fully informed and to be entertained. Even the immigrant press knew that it was an agency of assimilation; the newspaper in Yiddish, German, or Italian knew that its basic function was to put itself out of business. Today, it's possible for a Spanish-speaking immigrant to get the latest news and plunge into the fantasy of *telenovelas* without even being literate in Spanish. The smartest and most ambitious among the immigrants will go to those language schools; a minority will not. Their children are another matter. Most studies show that the children of Spanish-speaking immigrants are learning English at the same rate as the Jews, the Italians, the Poles, and the Greeks. The immigrants themselves learn enough English to get paid; their children speak both languages; *their* children speak only English. Sometimes the process appears much slower, but that's only because the immigration wave is continuing.

But the principles underlying the immigration wave remain as true now as they were in the 1920s. And for the immigrants and their children, the newspaper will continue to have function and meaning—if editors and publishers are wise. The newspaper verifies what has been heard on radio or television or through word of mouth. It expands upon, and corrects, all those erratic early bulletins. Above all, if the newspaper is even semiconscious of the presence of such large numbers of immigrants, it serves them as a guide to America. To its realities. To its politics and sports and culture. To its pleasures and opportunities. To its past and future. The immigrants have already brought renewed health to many American cities, but they are essential to the continuing health of newspapers. Along with women, they present the greatest opportunity for growth. And they are not inhabitants of some distant star. They are here.

Permit me one parochial example. In New York, Stuyvesant High School is one of the city's elite educational institutions. For generations, this public school has educated the children of many Sweeneys. To get in, youngsters must pass tough entrance examinations. Virtually all graduates go on to college. Today, the student body is roughly 50 percent Asian. Thirty years ago, it would have been 50 percent Jewish. That is an exact measure of where we now stand, for these current students are the children of the new immigrants. And they are not alone. They are the elite, but there are kids like them in many other city schools. They are a splendid part of the city's present tense.

They are also readers. If New York's tabloids treat them as if they are stupid, interested only in scandal and sensation, they will be lost as readers of those newspapers. They will choose to read the *New York Times*. They will turn to the Internet. These young people are not solemn nerds, humorless and narrow, but rather are conscious of the enormous opportunities laid out before them. They intend to seize the day. In addition, most of them want to honor the grinding sacrifices made by their parents. Those parents are serious people. Their heads are not filled with trivialities; they are too busy working. Their children want more than half-baked news about Donald Trump, Marv Albert, and Princess Di. Such young people do not often choose to get dumber.

If newspapers are to attract and hold these younger readers, they must have a vision, too. Joseph Pulitzer had one. In an age when amateur publishers and fearful or lazy editors keep putting out yesterday's paper, some of Pulitzer's words are worth repeating: "The newspaper that is true to its highest mission will concern itself with the things that *ought to happen tomorrow*, or next month, or next year, and will seek to make what ought to be come to pass."[8]

5

News Is a
Verb

A NY VISIT TO an American newsstand will illustrate the most widespread phenomenon of the times: The print media are runny with the virus of celebrity. The names and faces of movie actors, rock musicians, rappers, and fashion models adorn the covers of most magazines. If the subjects are not people who perform for a living, they are people whose celebrity is derived from notoriety. Depending upon the week or the year, Madonna competes with Joey Buttafuoco. Hugh Grant duels with Lorena Bobbitt. Eddie Murphy is cast beside the parents of JonBenet Ramsey. When accomplishment predates notoriety, the names are even bigger. Hey, folks, here's O. J. Simpson! And Marv Albert! And Frank Gifford! Big names, folks. Bigger than you insignificant schnooks! Bigger than God!

Newspapers are not immune to the celebrity virus. Depending upon the editors, they peddle a blander or coarser version of the same obsession with big names.

True accomplishment is marginal to the recognition factor. There is seldom any attention paid to scientists, poets, educators, or archaeologists. Citizens who work hard, love their spouses and children, pay taxes, give to charities, and break no laws are never in a newspaper unless they die in some grisly murder. Even solid politicians, those who do the work of the people without ambitions for immense power, and do so without scandal, are ignored. The focus of most media attention, almost to the exclusion of all other subjects, are those big names.

Newspaper reporters and editors know that most of these people aren't worth six minutes of anybody's time. Privately, they sneer at them or shrug them off. But they and their publishers are convinced that the mass audience is demanding these stories, so they keep churning them out. They defend their choices by insisting they are only giving the people what they want. If they are right, the country is in terrible trouble. I think they're wrong.

Newspaper people have more reason than others to know that some of these big names are mere creatures of hype and self-promotion. After all, they take the calls that are soon eagerly converted into stories. One entire subgenre flows from the jowly megalomania of New York real estate operator Donald Trump. There are many real estate people of more solid achievement and greater power than Trump's, and certainly many more accomplished businessmen. But such men and women usually prefer to live outside the spotlight; like people who really have money or those with truly interesting sex lives, they don't brag about them. They don't invent their lives in cahoots with press agents; they live them.

But Trump flies to the spotlight, even demands it. His motto seems to be "I'm written about, therefore I exist." He personally telephones gossip columnists and reporters to present them with stories about the wonders of himself, his great love life, his brusque divorces. In the spirit of true collaboration, the newspapers quote "sources close to Trump" as their authority, a code known to other editors and reporters but not revealed to the readers. In a way, Trump has his own brilliance. He has a genius for self-inflation, for presenting an illusion of accomplishment that often becomes the accomplishment itself. A tiny solar system now revolves around Trump's own self-created persona: his ex-wives, Ivana Trump and Marla Maples Trump, followed by his poor teenage daughter, Ivanka Trump, who as I write is being hurled into the world of fashion models under the benevolent gaze of Daddy. This vulgar saga threatens to go on and on.

No offense against taste is beyond Trump and his journalistic collaborators. Months after the death of Diana Spencer in a car wreck in Paris, Trump was publishing another of his ghostwritten hardcover hymns to his own genius. He gave an interview to the *New York Daily News*, which was serializing this book, even though most editors knew it was a second-rate exercise in self-promotion. Trump knew exactly what the publishers of the *Daily*

News wanted, and the next day's front page showed his face, his book, and a nauseating headline that screamed "I WISH I HAD DATED DI."

When I was editing the *Daily News*, I tried to control the virus of which Trump was the local symbol. Trump was not banned from the newspaper, but he did have to *do* something to appear in its pages. The "stories" slowed to a trickle, and one result was that we were beaten by the *New York Post* on the story of Trump's divorce. We had a rumor; they had Trump, speaking as a "source close to Trump." It was my responsibility and I chose not to run an unverified rumor. I was glad I made that choice. After I was canned, Trump "stories" came back in a fetid rush.

Trump is virtually a genre now. But another genre has been dominating the tabloids and other newspapers in the last year. I call it necrojournalism—the journalism of dead, or near-dead, celebrities. Princess Di was the greatest example of the genre. Certainly her death demanded extensive coverage. But after the known facts had been printed, the mysteries of the car crash defined, the paparazzi accused, and then the drunken limo driver, conveniently dead, arraigned in the public dock, the coverage kept on going. And it swiftly degenerated into a flood of mindless, sentimental custard. The funeral played live, the Elton John tune was thrown at us over and over and over again, the brother was hauled out and then her kids and then Prince Charles and the Queen and an endless parade of other royal unemployables. We didn't bury Franklin Roosevelt this way. The British didn't do this for Winston Churchill. Somewhere in the middle of this maudlin orgy, Mother Teresa, another celeb, died, but somehow she became a long footnote to the Princess Di story. Finally, this Olympics of emotion— some of it genuine and most of it fraudulent—was over. Most people scrubbed away at the grimy film of bathos; some must have been vaguely ashamed; others remained baffled by it all. But the stories kept coming. Long after the emotions were spent, necrojournalism was in full command. Newspapers serialized books about Princess Di. There were stories about how "brave" her kids were. There were stories implying that Princess Di, all by herself, stopped the spread of land mines. There were stories claiming that she was planning to marry Dodi and stories denying that she was going to marry Dodi. There were stories wondering who the hell Dodi was. Still it kept coming: accounts of planned Princess Di movies and Princess Di postage stamps and Princess Di memorials in England. And *still* it wasn't over. At the end of the year, there were even *more* special supplements. The *Daily News* in New York ran a total of thirty-five pages on Princess Di in its final Sunday paper of the year.

Meanwhile, there seemed to be a collective judgment that death sells—or, rather, that the deaths of famous people will sell. More examples of necrojournalism filled the narrow space between Princess Di stories. We read page-one stories about Marilyn Monroe, dead for thirty-five years; John F. Kennedy, dead for thirty-four years; Jacqueline Onassis, dead for four years; Frank Sinatra, nearly dead (as contrary as ever, he refused to die); Marv Albert, whose career was dead; and of course, Trump, who was brain-dead. The great fear in certain newspaper city rooms was that Sinatra, Ronald Reagan, Bob Hope, Boris Yeltsin, and the Pope would all die on the same day. To match the space given to Princess Di, they'd need to add 160 pages in special supplements alone.

Please don't misunderstand. As a newspaperman and a reader, I'm not against celebrity journalism; it just must be *journalism*. The profiles that run in *Vanity Fair*, the *New Yorker*, *GQ*, *Esquire*, and *People* are journalism. For the most part, the reporters devote time to understanding the subjects of their portraits. They take nothing for granted and make no a priori assumptions; if they begin the reporting admiring the big name and come to despise him, they tell that story. If they start with contempt and finish with admiration, they tell that story, too. They begin by poring over all previous stories about the big name, looking for patterns, contradictions, flaws, and strengths. They understand that any interview granted by a celebrity is itself a kind of performance, not evidence of anything authentic. It is commerce, part of the selling of a movie, a TV show, or an album. The good reporters know that a transient fifteen-minute interview in a hotel room during a big name's promotional tour is not really an interview. It is time pried out of the big name's tight schedule, the reporter taking his turn between two other interviewers who are gnawing at the soggy mound of cheese Danish in an outer room. It can be the *beginning* of journalism; it is seldom the end.

Serious journalists don't usually engage in this empty ritual. They need to spend extended time with the subject, like a fly on the wall, seeing what the big name actually *does*, in contrast to what he *says* he does. They attempt to make a rounded character out of the big name by discovering the origins of his or her art or craft, the often complicated or tortuous route that was taken to fame. They interview numerous sources among the subject's friends and enemies, parents and siblings, fellow professionals and old teachers, children, ex-wives or former husbands, and discarded lovers. The point of all this work is not to dish dirt, but to make intelligent connections between the life and the art.

A good writer of celebrity profiles follows in a fine tradition. Lytton Strachey's *Eminent Victorians* should be the model for the form: The pieces are well researched, witty, intelligent, and add to our understanding not only of the human beings sitting for Strachey's pen but of the era to which they belonged. From St. Clair McKelway to Gay Talese, Lillian Ross to David Halberstam, Joseph Mitchell to Richard Ben Cramer, journalists have shown how varied, powerful, and humane the form can be, and how it can help us understand our own times—in some rare cases, ourselves.

Most of the finest writers of big-name profiles work in other forms of journalism; they have covered wars, or sports, or foreign affairs. Jimmy Breslin, for example, is one of the greatest of all newspaper columnists; he has also written superb profiles. David Remnick was a fine foreign correspondent for the *Washington Post*; he also gives us profiles in the *New Yorker* that always enlarge our understanding of the subjects. Such journalists are properly humble about what they are doing. Because they have had wide experience of the real world, they have a sense of proportion about the big names. They have no interest in being publicists but are not afraid to celebrate human beings who have added something valuable to the world. They are also uninterested in working as hangmen, and for the same reason: that sense of proportion. They know that no profile can ever go as deeply into the secret places of the human heart as great fiction can. People lie to themselves as well as to others. The journalist is always a prisoner of what he or she is told. The truth is always elusive. But a proper humility on the part of reporters doesn't prevent the making of fine portraits.

That level of celebrity journalism certainly belongs in newspapers, even if it requires a series of articles. The examination of individual celebrities can tell us something about celebrity itself and how it functions in the collective American imagination. It can help readers to understand what they are really looking at when they go to a play or a movie or park in front of a TV set. It can offer guides to young people who are trying to make their own lives. When the reporting and writing are themselves examples of quality, as solidly constructed and handsomely designed as a Mercedes, a subtler message is also conveyed: Quality matters, and this newspaper is a quality product.

Quality is not demonstrated when space is turned over to press agents or when press agents are allowed to dictate the limits of an interview. Quality is not served by publishing unsubstantiated rumors based on single sources. Quality is not honored when a "profile" is the result of one brief interview and a tour of the clips (there is, of course, plenty of room in a newspaper for the one-on-one interview, clearly labeled as such; but the level of the questions must be high, and the interviewer must listen to what is being said by the big name in order to keep moving the talk to a deeper level). Quality is not enforced when significant news stories are deleted, cut to the bone, or shoved into the back of the paper to make room for a photograph of some big name going shopping.

Every celebrity story should be subjected to the same standards applied to stories of crime or politics. Celebrities didn't surrender their constitutional or legal rights when they began to practice their various crafts. It's evidence of naïveté or ignorance to say, "Well, they wanted to be rich and famous, and the paparazzi are part of the price they pay." I've known dozens of actors and actresses over the course of a reasonably long life; virtually none of them had as their primary goal the acquisition of fame and money. Later, as agents and managers and flacks begin to surround them, often cutting them off from "normal" life, fame and money can become more important. But even then, most of them just want the chance to do better and better work. Successful movies help in that ambition because more parts become available to choose from; but they don't get those parts by getting photographed on a nude beach or at a theater opening with a girlfriend.

To qualify as news, celebrities must *do* something. Not only that, they must do something that is surprising, interesting, or new. Mr. Big Name browsing in the Gap among the piles of jeans is not news. If Mr. Big Name throws the former Mrs. Big Name under the Sixth Avenue bus, that is news. Ms. Big Name sitting with friends in a restaurant is not news. If Ms. Big Name takes a job as a salesclerk at Saks, that is news. The proper noun is not enough; there must be a verb.

It is absolutely valid for a newspaper to report on big names when they get arrested, divorced, trampled by crazed fans, run over by taxis, or killed. Those are verbs to respect. It might even be news when a big name is given a ticket for speeding on some highway at midnight; it is just not *important* news and can be run as a box in the back of the newspaper. But large or small, the stories must be journalism. The most popular celebrity genre is also the most dangerous: the big name in trouble. Newspapers must ensure that the stories are true, or as close to truth as the imperfect tools of reporting can make them. They must be multiply sourced, not completely dependent upon versions of the event presented by cops or prosecutors. These days, newspapers should be very wary of charges of a sexual nature. If a woman's name is shielded by law, the celebrity is particularly vulnerable; basic fairness demands that the charges—and the person making them—be scrutinized in the toughest possible way. One basic rule of journalism is: *Things ain't always what they seem to be.* Even more important, perhaps, is this one: *If you want it to be true, it usually isn't.*

To guard against destroying the reputation of a celebrity, and the credibility of the newspaper itself, editors must be more cautious than ever. Every editor would be wise to mount in the city room large photographs of Richard Jewell, the security guard convicted by the press of the bombing at the 1996 Olympics, and Michael Irvin and Erik Williams of the Dallas Cowboys, convicted in the press of sexually assaulting a young woman. Both stories, as first presented, turned out to be dead wrong. Jewell collected a bundle of money from media organizations as a result. Another maxim that all readers should remember: *In the first twenty-four hours of a big story, about half the facts are wrong.* And editors must also keep clearly in mind that charges are not investigations; investigations are not indictments; indictments are not convictions.

The celebrity virus has infected many people who are supposed to be more neutral. This is the age of the prosecutor, not the defense attorney. Thirty years ago, Perry Mason served as counsel for the defense in the

American imagination. Now TV shows glorify the cops and the prosecutors. And real-life prosecutors, like real-life cops, watch these shows. They also look at television news. They read the newspapers. They see what editors believe is important. If a legal process can be transformed into a drama with a basic conflict, white hats up against black hats, they will make it into the newspapers. If they can assemble enough facts, no matter how circumstantial or spurious, to indict a big name, they will be famous. There will be a chance of cashing in the greatest of all American lotto tickets, the book deal (in the O. J. Simpson murder trial, the prosecutor, who lost, made a bigger score than the defense attorney, who won). Beyond that, they can run for higher office: In the world of celebrity, anything is possible.

Newspapers shouldn't be feeding this process. One of their roles in an era when fact keeps blending with or imitating fiction should be to separate myth from reality. And yet those myths are powerful. When I was a kid, I was as susceptible to the movie version of the newspaperman myth as any cop or prosecutor is to his or her own myth. At least once a year, I still watch the video of *Deadline U.S.A.*, with Humphrey Bogart as the tough, fearless editor of a dying (of course!) newspaper; it reminds me of the emotions and ambitions that drew me to the newspaper business in the first place. I know that there is a vast gap between a wonderful fiction and the practice of a difficult craft, but if we don't recognize the myths that drive us, we get in trouble. That recognition should make us all pause. Kenneth Starr, in his obsessive pursuit of Bill Clinton, should have wondered if he was becoming Inspector Javert of *Les Misérables.*

Still, the myths can be useful. One article of faith in the reporter's myth is that we must let the chips fall where they may. We are not fans. We can't write about big names as if we were looking for autographs. We can't take an active part in the process of turning prosecutors into big names in return for that curse of the reporting craft, *access.* It is better to lose a story than to become an unpaid flack for any public figure. When there are undisclosed factors in the relationships between reporters and the people they cover, the reader is being cheated. Eventually, the swindle becomes clear and credibility is a casualty.

Long-term credibility must always be considered when editors decide how to cover the professional activities of big names. The way a story is played, the space awarded to it, and the tone of the text are all messages to the readers. Just because the Spice Girls are the show-business phenomenon of the month, newspapers are not obliged to hand-deliver page after breathless page to the act's publicity machine. Let them buy ads. Certainly there is room in the features section to explain how the act was created and cast, to explain that it did not grow organically from shared friendships and love of music. Editors can ask reporters to make well-defined parallels to similarly concocted show-business acts, from the Monkees and Menudo to the silicone glories of *Baywatch.*

They can underline the differences, too. It is legitimate to look at the Spice Girls as a triumph of marketing, not art. Psychologists can discuss the phenomenon, lyrics can be analyzed. But all must be within the broad context of hard reporting. Newspapers are not in the business of selling CDs; to do so in the guise of reporting news is a form of consumer fraud. To simply run pictures of five hot babes, with text that sounds like advertising copy, is a form of journalistic lip-synching.

The typical publisher's reply to such complaints would be a combination of three sentences: (1) "Lighten up"; (2) "Who does it hurt?" and (3) "The readers can't get enough of these chicks." But hard reporting doesn't have to be written with a heavy hand; telling the story of a show-business act doesn't have to sound like a report on the civil war in Rwanda. Lightness of touch is a great gift. But newspaper stories that are simpleminded, cheap, mindless, and trivial *can* be hurtful. They hurt the credibility of the newspaper. When publicity handouts are dressed up as stories and crowd out real reporting on education, politics, or the environment, hurt is done to the entire newspaper. It becomes thinner; its spine of substance is weakened; it looks as if it is pandering. And we don't really know if such stories, done this way, *are* what the readers want. In a variety of polls, readers have said what they want: ongoing scrutiny of public officials; news about education, the environment, and their own communities. Everything else is of much less interest, including gossip and celebrity reporting. But if an editor cites these studies to a publisher, the publisher usually replies, "That's because they're ashamed to admit they like this stuff." In my experience, publishers have almost no direct contact with the readers and have no way of knowing whether such an assumption is true. But if it *were* true, then why waste money on expensive polls? The money could be better spent on hiring reporters. And if the publishers are right about what readers want, why is circulation at so many newspapers stagnant or in decline?

Again, one reason for reader indifference is content. Loading down a newspaper with trivialities at the expense of substance sends out a clear message: The reader is dumb, or at least a little simple. And as a simpleton, says the logic of the assumption, the reader has an endless appetite for shit. Publishers and editors who wouldn't consider for a minute the purchase of a third-rate car or a third-rate suit of clothes are too often engaged in making a third-rate product of their own and knowingly sending it out to the public. Sooner or later, the reader wises up. Sometimes sooner. Always later.

In any popular newspaper, there must be room for stories that are light or funny, about subjects that are less than earthshaking. In the same way, in a department store, there is room for toys and games, not just apparel and appliances. These stories can be done with high style. They can be sassy. They can make a city laugh. But they just have to be journalism. At their core, they too must have an interesting verb. There can't be different standards in different sections of the same newspaper.

The reader doesn't finish with the news section and then accept that everything else is less than true. The readers want to believe that it's *all* true. It's just not all of the same importance. Put the Spice Girls on page three and the story of the cuts in library funds on page twenty-eight and you are making a statement about relative importance. You are also making a comment about those readers you so desperately want and for whom you have such utter contempt.

6

-30-

I WANT TO believe that all newspapers have a future. If they disappear, the country will be diminished, and for all its grievous sins and terrible flaws, this remains one hell of a sweet country. As I write, young men and women are carrying rifles into the mountains of distant countries, prepared to die for freedoms we take for granted. From the days when we were a colony and then right through the history of the Republic, newspapers have been essential to the American idea. As concrete examples of freedom, they were the essential instruments of American reform. They measured the promises of the Constitution against the sometimes evil and unjust realities of American life and forced the country to change. As we continue the long, heartbreaking process of becoming better versions of ourselves, newspapers will, I hope, continue to be the point of the spear. They should enable us, in the phrase of Albert Camus, to love our country, and justice, too.

But I fear for the future. The opportunities to build circulation among women and immigrants are being ignored, or given only sporadic or mechanical attention. The content of newspapers is being coarsened and cheapened. Instead of being the medium that corrects, verifies, or debunks the farrago of fact and rumor that is passed along by the Internet, we are merely passing it along ourselves. Instead of doing what television can't do, we are trying to become printed television.

There are some very good newspapers in the country, offering a combination of quality reporting and intelligent services. They will survive. But I don't really want to live in a country where the only newspapers left standing are the *New York Times*, the *Washington Post*, the *Wall Street Journal*, and the *Los Angeles Times*. That is too much power to place in the hands of too few people.

I want more newspapers, not fewer. I want them to cut their prices, to attract more readers at the low end of the economic curve. I want their stories to be better-reported and better-written. They can be irreverent, sassy, and bright, but they also have to be true. I want the design to be handsome and accessible. I want them to be fun. I don't care if their editorial pages are liberal or conservative, I just want a straight count in the news pages, illumination in the features pages, and a sense of drama and celebration in the sports pages. Nobody can speak for all Americans. But I think those desires are shared by the majority of people in this country.

In my time as a New Yorker and a newspaperman, I

have witnessed the deaths of nine local newspapers: *PM,* the *Star,* the *Compass,* the *Brooklyn Eagle,* the *Daily Mirror,* the *New York Herald Tribune,* the *New York Journal American,* the *World-Telegram and Sun,* and the *World Journal Tribune,* which was a composite of the last three. I went to some of their wakes and said good-bye to men and women who had given their lives to the newspaper business and were now leaving it forever. They were some of the best people I've ever known.

Those bitter rituals, charged with sad, grieving anger, were not unique to New York. They were repeated in too many cities all over the nation. And it is no accident that many of the cities that buried newspapers have never themselves been the same. Healthy cities are essential to newspapers, but healthy newspapers are also essential to cities. They supply a context for individual lives. They record change and offer visions of the future. They separate facts from rumors. They are the place to which hundreds of thousands come every day for a sense of connection to others. They are our *zócalos.*

Because of all those deaths in the family, I am very aware of the need for newspapers to be successful businesses. But for me, and for thousands of professional newspapermen and women, there is only one sure way to make a newspaper a success: The publisher must make an absolute commitment to quality. That means hiring professional editors, with deep knowledge of their communities, who will have the freedom to run the news side of the newspaper. That is what Katharine Graham did with Ben Bradlee and the *Washington Post;* she was the publisher, he was the editor, together they made a good newspaper into a great one.

Again, I want to emphasize what should be obvious and often isn't, especially to many of those who own newspapers. The commitment to quality must permeate the *entire* newspaper. Reporters are the infantry of the news business; they must be hired intelligently; guided, directed, taught by older professionals; and rewarded for good work. In the news pages, the writing must be of the highest possible order: lucid, vivid, concrete, smart. Columnists, who have greater latitude than hard news reporters, and are paid to have opinions, should be encouraged to be surprising; too many columnists take their subjects off the rack and reach for an automatic sneer or a simpleminded insight. Features departments should be true guides for the readers, providing maps of the city's consciousness; in their pages, the writing can be more adventurous and rich, conveying with language the excitement of discovering what is new in the arts, medicine, science, health. All members of a staff should take some cues from the sports section; in most newspapers the best writing is done by sports columnists and reporters. Good reporting does not have to be boring. Even the comic sections should become havens of quality. There should be term limits for certain mindless strips and panels; too many are written and drawn by people who have never even met the creators, who are long gone. There need to be fresher strips, as good as

Bill Watterson's late, lamented *Calvin and Hobbes,* and fewer strips that are run larger.

Quality newspapers now have a powerful new role to play, one that should guarantee health and growth well into the next century. They must do what television news and the Internet cannot do, or choose not to do: provide knowable facts to a large audience and separate the knowable from the speculative. In the age of information overload, newspapers must be the medium that people believe. They don't have to be first. They can even be last. *But they must be right.*

In my experience, virtually all editors, reporters, writers, and photographers want to do good work for good newspapers. They are not the problem. The problem is a larger one, most of which derives from the publishers. Too many publishers think of newspapermen, including their own editors, as hopeless romantics, committed to the myth of the fearless journalist. They are actually right. But they should trust that myth. Upon that myth, they can build great newspapers that will also be healthy businesses. Newspapers need men and women with fire in the belly, not a collection of bloodless bureaucrats, content to clerk the news.

Trust is the heart of the matter. Publishers must trust their editors. Editors must trust their reporters. All must trust the intelligence and good sense of their readers. When such overlapping acts of trust and faith are absent or shrugged off, the newspaper usually goes downscale and keeps going all the way to the bottom of the grave.

This is always done in the name of giving the people what they want. By the time publishers realize that the readers want a newspaper that is a whole lot better, it's too late.

At the end of a tumultuous century, the opportunities are now here for publishers and newspapermen to build the newspapers of the immediate future. The effort will require intelligence, patience, trust, and, yes, some of that romantic spirit. But I have to believe that if the effort is made, newspapers will flourish, and that will be good for all of us, men and women, citizens and immigrants. If newspapers do what only they can do, we will have better cities, better citizens, and a smarter, more humane country. At the very least, we will have avoided adding anything more to the appalling history of human lousiness.

Notes

INTRODUCTION

1. For a superb account of this trend, see Doug Underwood, *When MBAs Rule the Newsroom,* Columbia University Press, 1993.

2. "Press Flawed, News Chiefs Admit," *Editor and Publisher,* Jan. 17, 1998. The poll was conducted for the magazine by the Technometrica Institute of Policy and Politics.

3. For numbers that include wire services, magazines, and broadcast media, see Peter Braestrup, "Epilogue," in *The Future of News,* edited by Philip S. Cook, Douglas Gomery, and Lawrence W. Lichty, Woodrow Wilson Center Press, Johns Hopkins University Press, 1992. Obviously, such numbers are subject to additions and subtractions. But newspapers still employ more journalists than all other media combined.

4. Underwood, *When MBAs Rule the Newsroom,* p. xiv. William B. Blankenberg, in *The Future of News,*

says that households increased 40 percent for the same period, while Leo Bogart, in the same volume, states that households increased by 44.5 percent from 1970 to 1988. They all make the same basic point: Newspapers are not keeping pace with growth in population of households.

CHAPTER 4

1. W. A. Swanberg, *Pulitzer,* Scribner, 1967, p. 70.

2. Ibid., p. 96.

3. Ibid., p. 97.

4. By 1939, the Sunday circulation was about 3 million, largest in the *world.* The daily sold about 2.3 million. In 1997, after television, strikes, changes in ownership, the circulation was at about 800,000 on Sundays, 720,000 daily, still the fourth largest circulation in the United States.

5. John Chapman, *Tell It to Sweeney: The Informal History of the New York Daily News,* Doubleday, 1961, p. 136. See also Leo E. McGivena and others, *The News: The First Fifty Years of New York's Picture Newspaper,* News Syndicate Co., 1969.

6. Chapman, *Tell It to Sweeney,* p. 137.

7. Ibid., p. 142.

8. Swanberg, *Pulitzer,* p. 96.

ABOUT THE AUTHOR

PETE HAMILL has been a newspaperman for almost four decades. Starting at the *New York Post* in 1960, he has worked at several newspapers as a reporter, rewriteman, war correspondent, and columnist. Most recently, he served as editor in chief of the *New York Daily News*. He has also written for almost all major American magazines. In addition to his journalism, he is the author of eight novels, including the bestselling *Snow in August,* two collections of short stories, two anthologies of his journalism, and the memoir *A Drinking Life.* He also has written many screenplays. Hamill is married to the Japanese journalist Fukiko Aoki and is the father of two daughters. He lives in New York City.

A Note on The Library of Contemporary Thought

This exciting new monthly series tackles today's most provocative, fascinating, and relevant issues, giving top opinion makers a forum to explore topics that matter urgently to themselves and their readers. Some will be think pieces. Some will be research oriented. Some will be journalistic in nature. The form is wide open, but the aim is the same: to say things that need saying.

**Look for these titles coming soon from
The Library of Contemporary Thought**

CARL HIAASEN

TEAM RODENT
How Disney Devours America

SEYMOUR HERSH

AGAINST ALL ENEMIES
Gulf War Syndrome: The War
between America's Ailing Veterans
and Their Government

EDWIN SCHLOSSBERG

INTERACTIVE EXCELLENCE
Defining and Developing New
Standards for the Twenty-first Century

ANNA QUINDLEN

HOW READING CHANGED MY LIFE